Dear Gene -

Good news. But - sorry it's a boy -

Getting your letters regularly and do what is necessary
at this end -

How are you paying our bills? I mean in what form, I mean,
since I have no bank account. We will have to open one, of a kind, for the Foundation when I
return which will be soon now.

I think you would get what you can together of the cost of
running the farm before I turned it over to thee. Say
the last year or two - You probably have something -
Wages Taxes Etc.

We never got much more than milk, eggs butter garden-stuff
for the Fellowship - out of it. Sold calves and pigs - but no
record probably.

And probably no use making one except to show how well
off we were when we had nothing -
I want to see where I was and where I am, that's all.
and get back to independence of all fixed charges for upkeep
so far as possible - Working toward that from now on.
To do it intelligently we must get as accurate a survey
as we can - of what led up to the FOUNDATION

I don't know what you have on record - Let's have
what you've got. Your memory is no better than mine,
Things are about as usual here. Weather wonderful -
Olgivanna brown as a berry - but still very nervous.
She seems to take to the camp again - like the heroine
she is -

My love to all the boys - and girls -

All is not lost - yet -

Affection F. LL W.

Did you get a telegram from me
asking you to send selection of ten
mounted vertical Kodaslips.
And a selection of ten from unmounted
pile?
If not send them once, post at once.

LETTERS TO APPRENTICES

FRANK LLOYD WRIGHT

Selected and with commentary

by

Bruce Brooks Pfeiffer

The Press
at
California State University, Fresno

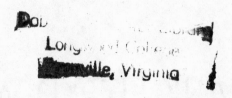

Dedicated to Mrs. Frank Lloyd Wright, but for whom the Taliesin Fellowship would have had neither past nor future.

ACKNOWLEDGMENTS

For permission to use the photographs in this volume, my grateful thanks to the following:

Allen Lape Davison: *Taliesin West against the McDowell Mountains.*

John Engstead: *Hillside drafting room, Mr. and Mrs. Wright.*

Yukio Futagawa: *The Solomon R. Guggenheim Museum, Marin County Civic Center.*

Hedrich-Blessing: *Studio at Taliesin, Fallingwater.*

Valentino Sarra: *Sunday evening concert in the Taliesin living room.*

Edmund Teske: *Birthday party in the Taliesin living room.*

The Frank Lloyd Wright Foundation: *Taliesin North early winter, Hillside, Constructing Taliesin West, Taliesin West, Taliesin chamber ensemble, Broadacre City - schematic plan, Herbert Jacobs house, George Sturges house, Crystal Heights Project, Masieri Memorial Project, Rogers Lacy Hotel Project, Pittsburgh Point Triangle Community and Civic Center Project, Boulder House Project, San Francisco Bridge Project, Lenkurt Electric Project.*

Quotations from Frank Lloyd Wright, *An Autobiography* are reprinted by permission of the publisher, Horizon Press, from *An Autobiography* by Frank Lloyd Wright © 1977, New York and by permission of the copyright owner, The Frank Lloyd Wright Foundation.

Cover design from a Taliesin Fellowship brochure by Eugene Masselink.

CONTENTS

PREFACE

The letters in this volume are the first published collection of the correspondence of Frank Lloyd Wright. They concern the Taliesin Fellowship, that group of young men and women who were his apprentices from 1932 to 1959. Throughout those years many hundreds of Taliesin Fellows arrived, to come into contact with the greatness of the world's foremost architect. They stayed for varying periods of time: a year, several years, a decade; some came and chose to remain at Taliesin for a lifetime. Each has left an imprint upon the life of Taliesin, and the letters that Mr. Wright wrote to his apprentices recapture memories that surround each of them. But most important, his letters provide an intimate view of Frank Lloyd Wright himself, in personal situations that only letters can reveal.

In the archives of the Frank Lloyd Wright Foundation are some 1400 letters and telegrams to apprentices. Several thousand more concern the life of the Fellowship and its operation. Published chronologically, along with the necessary documentation and explanations, these could provide a mass of material for further scholarly research. We intend eventually to publish the entire correspondence in this format.

The present volume, however, has a more immediate aim: it seeks to recapture the experiences, emotions, trials, errors, and triumphs of the Taliesin Fellowship. To do so most vividly, a few hundred letters have been strategically selected and grouped together under four main headings, each group proceeding from the early years to the later ones.

First, there is the growth and development of the idea of education at Taliesin; next there are the details of daily life at Taliesin, giving substance to the idea as reality; then there are the personal relations with Mr. Wright, often as complex and compelling as the man himself; and finally there are those letters written to apprentices concerning their participation in the architectural work of Frank Lloyd Wright.

Besides those four groups there are an introduction, a brief history of the Fellowship, and a concluding group that contains some letters from the apprentices themselves describing the profound influence Taliesin had upon their work and their lives.

Throughout the text Mr. Wright's highly individual method of writing and punctuating has, for the most part, been retained so as not to lose the flavor and character of his letters. He wrote longhand, always, and then the letters were typed with special care so as to duplicate his originals. Instead of the conventional P.S., he employed N.B. (*nota bene*). He had a consistent and typical way of using quotation marks. But by far his favorite individual punctuation mark was the hyphen, to indicate what might be described, in the nomenclature of music, as a *fermata*, a considered pause. Many of his letters are "conversational," and often when he saw the written text of something that he had said in speaking, taken down verbatim, he remarked that what was conspicuously lacking on the printed page was the twinkle in the corner of his eye.

In the selection, arrangement, and editing of these letters I am grateful for personal and valuable help from other members of the Frank Lloyd Wright Foundation. Working with them has been an act of intense reflection; we found ourselves frequently inundated by powerful memories of our beloved Mr. Wright.

Mrs. Wright, who owns the first publication rights to all her husband's letters, sanctioned and encouraged this work from its very start one year ago. My gratitude to her, as the strongest inspiring force in my life today, could never be adequately expressed.

B.B.P.
Taliesin West   October 1982

I

THE TALIESIN FELLOWSHIP

At a time in life when most men would consider retirement and the closing down of their careers, Frank Lloyd Wright at age 63 was the most creative of all architects and unquestionably the pioneer in his profession. His work had already achieved enormous impact. No factor, form, or feature of modern architecture built or conceived in the previous four decades was without its roots and inspiration in the work he had begun in 1893 on the prairies surrounding Chicago and in its suburbs. He had destroyed the age-old cliche of the box in architecture by liberating space. He was the first to build on the concept that the space within was the reality of the building, not its four walls and ceiling. The Chinese mystic Lao-Tzu had taught this concept some 2500 years ago; Frank Lloyd Wright was the first to build it. Moreover, he created an architecture indigenous to the twentieth century in keeping with the technology of modern machines, mechanical developments, and new materials, without ever losing sight of the human being and human scale. His forms were as varied as the multitudinous solutions he propounded--solutions for every type and kind of design fitted to the requirements of contemporary mankind. Had his life ended at the age of 63, in 1932, history would even then have regarded him and his work as among the most prodigious and the most creative in the vast review of man's recorded accomplishments during the past 6000 years.

Yet he was to live another 27 years, to the age of 90. He was to create designs for buildings—some completed, many others left as projects—of such hitherto unimagined space and form, of such breadth of beauty, as to make us wonder how this productivity, this creativity, this immense variety could spring forth from the mind and heart of but one man.

1932 was one of the worst periods in American history. The collapse of the financial fabric of the nation, some three years before, had thrust the country into widespread bankruptcy. Very few survived untouched, and the government had to step in to bail out an ailing economy. Architecture had fairly well come to a halt, with some isolated exceptions. Most major building projects were sponsored by the government, and governments, like conservative monied interests, rarely invest in the innovative, the creative, the visionary. Instead they choose timeworn designs and standards. The United States, in the thirties, was dedicated to the Colonial, to the Greek revival, and to the styles and tastes of European cultures already 500 years dead, styles totally anachronistic to the needs and conditions of the twentieth century.

By 1932 several large projects undertaken by Frank Lloyd Wright came to a halt. Among these were a luxurious resort hotel for Arizona, an apartment building for Los Angeles, a group of three apartment towers in New York, another group of connected or grouped apartment towers in Chicago, a school for the Rosenwald Foundation in La Jolla, California, an office building for a newspaper in Oregon. Several other projects were in the initial stages: a luxury house, "the House on the Mesa," for Denver, Colorado; a new concept for gas stations; and three projects for theaters in Woodstock, New York. All were to remain projects only.

Two residential works, however, were designed and constructed: a large house for Mr. Wright's cousin, Richard Lloyd Jones, in Tulsa, and a summer home on Lake Erie for Darwin D. Martin of the Larkin Company. Both of these were started in 1929 and were to be the last commissions carried to completion until 1934.

At this time of his life, when his constantly expanding genius was about to create a succession of buildings in a steady progression of new ideas, Mr. Wright's devoted wife, Olgivanna Lloyd Wright, suggested founding a school for the training of young architects at their house, Taliesin. But the Taliesin Fellowship—as they named it—would not be a school in the conventional sense.

Mr. Wright's ancestors immigrated from Wales to southern Wisconsin and established their lives in a valley bordered by gentle rolling hills. The word Taliesin is Welsh in origin, being the name of a famous Druid Bard who sang of the fine arts in the sixth century; the name means, "shining brow." When Mr. Wright built his home and studio on the brow of a lovely hill in this ancestral valley, he called it Taliesin. Constructed in 1911, it was twice partially destroyed by fire, once in 1914 and again in 1925. Each time it was rebuilt. The fires at Taliesin were a devastation from which not many men could recover, but Mr. Wright's spirit was actually strengthened by tragedy and hardship.

In 1949, on Mr. Wright's 80th birthday, several of us sat in the studio sharing breakfast with him, the room full of generous bowls of his favorite flowers, wild roses. He pointed to the entry way, where a small loggia separates the studio part of Taliesin from the living part, and said, "Each time the fire was stopped at that loggia and the studio was spared. It was as if God questioned my character, but never my work!"

In the same valley, a half mile away, Mr. Wright had designed and built a school building for his two maiden aunts, Jane and Ellen Lloyd Jones. They had begun, in 1885, a revolutionary educational center called the Hillside Home School, the first coeducational boarding school, grades 1 through 12, in the United States. Their buildings were among the most innovative of Mr. Wright's early work. Before their deaths they asked that somehow, in some way, he take over those buildings and use them for some educational venture. Thus, after 1932, the Hillside buildings, or Hillside as they came to be called, would become the main center for the activities of the Taliesin Fellowship. A gymnasium was converted into a playhouse-theater. The large kitchen and dining room served the Fellowship. Later a drafting room was added, with dormitory rooms running along each side. Hillside had originally included some farm buildings used in the days of the school, but those had been demolished, and on the slopes of another hill, half way between Taliesin and Hillside, a new farm group, called Midway, was built. Here were kept the farm animals, barns, silos and granaries, machine sheds and dairy. A charming little series of triangular huts ran down the hill to the lake's edge below for the hogs and pigs, which Mr. Wright liked to refer to as "Pork Avenue." Along the contours of the connecting hills were laid out the kitchen gardens for fresh vegetables, herbs, berries, and fruit.

The timeworn Beaux Arts tradition—washed across the ocean from Paris and entrenched in almost every architectural school in the nation—had proven one evident fact: it could not produce creative architects. The Taliesin Fellowship could and would, by rejecting the Old World's means and methods of education. Instead of students there would be "apprentices." Instead of classwork there would be learning by doing. The idea of apprenticeship appealed to Mr. Wright because it implied a working association, not a pedantic one. "Apprenticeship at Taliesin," he wrote, "is much where it was in feudal times with this important difference: an apprentice then was his master's slave; at Taliesin he is his master's comrade to any extent he qualifies himself to become one."

In the autumn of 1932 the text for the Taliesin Fellowship Brochure was completed and sent out across the country, explaining what this new architectural education was intended to be. It read as follows:

THE TALIESIN FELLOWSHIP IS AN EXTENSION OF ARCHITECTURE AT TALIESIN TO THE ARCHITECTURE OF MUSIC SCULPTURE AND PAINTING

BY WAY OF AGRICULTURE MANUFACTURE AND BUILDING TO IN-
CLUDE SEVENTY APPRENTICES AND SEVEN...

Frank Lloyd Wright, together with a leader who will be in residence
with the apprentices, four resident associates; a technical research man
in structural engineering, a sculptor, a painter and a musician together
with a group of seventy qualified apprentices, carefully chosen for the
work to be done and seven honor apprentices, paying no tuition,
selected by the Fellowship for qualifications of leadership. This group
assisted in the workshops by three technical research men, trained
engineers in industry, will constitute the membership of the Fellowship.

Leaders in the creative thought of our own and many other countries
have expressed the desire to come and share for a time in Fellowship activities when the provisions now being made for them are ready, residing
there, temporarily, to execute commissions.

Any rational attempt to integrate Art and Industry and correlate both
with everyday life in America must proceed as essential architecture. Our
Architecture can only grow by way of such social, industrial and
economic processes as are our own.

Not only will the framework and background of our future as a
civilization be erected as architecture in this organic sense, but the
qualities most worth while in any study of life whether as philosophy,
sculpture, painting or music are, fundamentally, architecture.

Architecture, therefore, that is of life itself, or from the ground up,
must be the first concern of any genuine culture. Work itself is indispen-
sable to any comprehension of the principles which underlie life and the
Arts alike. Art in any creative sense may be inculcated or cultured in
work but can not be taught by book.

An "alliance" between what we call Art and commercial Industry can
not be good enough because no mere "alliance", however useful, can
ever be creative. If organic forms appropriate to our life are to grow from
within and are to be, in themselves, worthwhile expressions of machine-
age life, the original work will be done where the workers themselves
not only have spontaneous recourse to practical, modern shop and
general working conditions but, at the same time, have the benefit of the
inspirational fellowship of genuinely creative artists in the work to be
done.

Whatever creative impulse has survived among us should somewhere, somehow have some fair chance at fresh life uncontaminated by
human expressions already dead or dying. Inasmuch as the city is a dying
formula, the Taliesin Fellowship lives and works in the country. Constant
contact with the nature of the ground and with nature-growth are the
most valuable "texts" in this connection when the contacts are forms of
experience directly related to creative work.

The Fellowship establishment practicing what it preaches, is a simple
expression of indigenous architecture. It is located on a State Highway in

Southern Wisconsin near the Wisconsin River, a two-hundred acre farm about forty miles from Madison and four miles from the nearest village.

In the life of the Fellowship, the harmonious integrity of the architectural circumstance is considered an important feature and although many of the buildings are already well along, every apprentice will have an active share in completing the establishment during the next several years.

The work in architecture at Taliesin, near by, during the past thirty years has proved itself and has gone far enough in the current of contemporary ideas throughout the world so that good work to improve the design of their buildings and the utilitarian objects they produce can now be done in co-operation with our more advanced producers and manufacturers.

As the Taliesin Fellowship our main purpose extends the apprenticeship from the seven or ten apprentices to which that work has been limited at Taliesin to include seventy-seven apprentices. Eventually all will work under the combined leadership of the inner-group as described, each apprentice actually at work, eventually, according to his or her own inclination, but with needed help, toward the machine-craft art of a machine-age life in this machine age.

A united effort to make such new forms as machine-work and modern-processes must have, if America is to have any natural life worth living, will be a constant practical aim of the whole work.

During the years past applications have come from all parts of the world from many young architects desiring to come to Taliesin to live and work.

This new Fellowship will enable seventy-seven to be immersed in the many-sided activities of Architecture in all its phases.

These activities, gradually and spontaneously as possible, will be extended to include work in all of the arts as, also, the various modern machine-crafts.

Working on various forms of practical enterprise in direct personal contact with the currents of modern thought and feeling, all demanding spiritual integrity in our new life, we believe many aspiring young artists will, here, find means to upbuild forces within themselves that will guarantee to us, as a people, a natural architecture.

We are beginning this work hoping to grow gradually but spontaneously from within, upon a free and individual basis, keeping our own independence; everyday life made healthy and fruitful by direct experience with idea as work and with work as idea: many-sided as that work may be.

The home life itself will be simple. Meals in common. Fixed hours for all work; recreation and sleep. Each worker will eventually have his or her own room for study and rest. Imaginative entertainment will be a feature of the home-life; plays, evenings with the literature of music, by way of Trio or Quartette, the cinema of our own and other countries and evening conferences to which musicians, literary men, artists, scientists will be invited and, sometimes, the public.

And the beautiful region is itself a never failing source of recreation.

Horseback riding will be encouraged, an adequate stable provided for a sufficient number of saddle horses.

The Fellowship work in all its branches will have as its motive the organic philosophy of an organic architecture for modern life as we are living that life at the present time, but some appropriate sense of the future seen as the present will give direction to every effort.

The study of architecture, the first year, will be taken, informally, into special studies of building design and building construction, typography, ceramics, woodwork and textiles. And this informal study will go hand in hand with characteristic model-making. Eventually it will go on with practical experiments in the machine-crafts as these experiments may be made by the apprentices in the workshop with modern-machinery and technical processes.

Apprenticeship will be the condition and should be the attitude of mind of the Fellowship workers. A fair division of all the labor in all the branches of the work will be the share of each individual although any individual's predilection for some particular art-expression will be encouraged.

There will be no age-limit as to the apprenticeship so long as the quality of youth is characteristic. But the special qualifications of each applicant—(good background and good correlation of faculties foremost among them)—will finally be decided upon by the leader of the Fellowship and Mr. Wright after a month's trial in actual Fellowship work.

The Fellowship aims, first, to develop a well-correlated, creative human being with a wide horizon but capable of concentration upon the circumstances in which he lives.

A preliminary requirement of each member of the Fellowship will be to learn to draw well what he sees as the best means to develop the necessary correlation of the faculties.

The Laboratories and machine workshops as well as several of the buildings are not yet ready but eventually all will be planted as planned, next to the living quarters, as shown in the accompanying drawings. The draughting room, assembly room, studio for painting, studio for sculpture, demonstrating rooms and the small theatre are already built.

The first experimental units to be put to work are those of architectural construction and design, research in technical industrial engineering, the philosophy of architecture, typographical design, and the printing of the publication that will be the organ of the Fellowship; molding and casting adopted to modern systems of construction in glass, concrete and metal; woodworking by modern machinery. A collateral but informal study of the philosophy and practice of sculpture, painting, drama and rhythm is essential for all apprentices. These first units are to be followed, as soon as possible, by the shopwork of actual glass-making, pottery, modern reproduction processes in many forms, as we may find the help to establish these units. Men of Industry in the United States will find it worth their while to co-operate with us in design research, each in their particular branch of manufacture.

After having had several years acquaintance with the actual performance of the apprentice, a personal testimonial will be given to each worker at the end of his or her apprenticeship, the length of the apprenticeship to be determined by the circumstances. During each working year a holiday of six weeks for each worker will be arranged, as the work may permit, and if the worker so desires.

Inasmuch as the Fellowship is not a "Foundation" but, to preserve direction, initiative and prompt action, is an individual, independent enterprise, the revenue for the first several years will come mainly from tuition fees and the sustaining work, four hours each day, of the apprentices. Added to this as the work grows may be compensation from industries for services rendered or to be rendered; the sale of completed art-objects; subscriptions to the various publications to be printed by the Fellowship and the contributions of "Fellowships"–(the equivalent of Scholarships)–as gifts, or gifts of equipment from "Friends of the Fellowship." The "Friends" to be a group organized among those who believe in our work and who are willing and able to add scope to our usefulness as the Fellowship grows.

The success of our experiment must depend upon the quality of our membership and upon the spirit of co-operation felt and practiced by fellowship members. The apprentices, alone, can make their apprenticeship fruitful.

Each apprentice is required to pay the fixed fee for tuition according to terms stated on the application blank herewith. In addition the apprentices will be required to do his or her share of work, four hours each day, in the upkeep and care of the grounds and buildings on the farm, for the privilege of participation in experimental work in the studios and shops and in the production of art-objects and practical exemplars for industry and buildings or for exhibition and, perhaps, sale. An account will be kept of the money thus had from all sales, and at the end of each year a fair dividend will be paid to each member of the Fellowship which in the course of a few years may materially reduce the tuition fee to be paid by the apprentices.

The farm and the various gardens into which it is divided will be so managed as to employ the help of the apprenticeship under skilled guidance so that not only will the apprentices gain practical experience in farming but a substantial portion of the living of the apprentices will come from their own labor on the ground, thus enabling the tuition fee to remain as it is now fixed.

FRANK LLOYD WRIGHT, TALIESIN, SPRING GREEN, WIS., JANUARY 1ST, 1933

Later, when Frank Lloyd Wright discussed this prospectus in *An Autobiography* he added:

"No sooner was this ambitious scheme proposed than we abandoned it. After sending out the circular we decided we would do better to stick to what we already had than to go too far institutional or 'educational'. I had certain qualifications; Olgivanna had others to add to mine. So we put our heads, as well as our hearts, together, simplified it all to come within our immediate capacities, so we thought, and wisely cut down possible membership to twenty-three. But the foregoing text—text by no means simple enough—was nevertheless sent out. It had the effect we hoped for and intended. Twenty-three young men and women brought twenty-three times six hundred and fifty dollars—one year each—to work it out at Taliesin. After, a fair cross section of Young America assembled there October 1, 1932, eager to go to work—ill prepared for anything except academic study of some sort. Least of all for the Freedom Taliesin had to offer."

Three basic fundamentals of training persisted from the very beginning: first, training in the art and craft of drawing by means of working on Mr. Wright's architectural work in the drafting room. Second, the knowledge of building techniques and construction methods by means of actually building, modifying, repairing, and remodeling Taliesin in Wisconsin, and later, from the ground up, the construction of Taliesin West in Arizona. Third, the knowledge of how to maintain a building—minor repairing, and decorating the buildings in which the Fellowship continues to live. Along with this third aspect were included the day to day routines of cooking, laundry, gardening, and all the work that is required to maintain life itself independent of hired help.

The only exception to the rule opposing the use of hired help was the hiring of an expert stone mason and a carpenter to help train the Fellowship members in these construction crafts. They usually were local men who had worked on the Hillside and Taliesin buildings for many years and understood the new type of stone masonry and woodwork details that these buildings first employed.

In December of 1936, following a severe attack of pneumonia Mr. Wright took Mrs. Wright and their daughter, Iovanna, to Arizona in search of property to buy. They had stayed in Arizona before, in 1927, during the work on the Arizona Biltmore Hotel, again in 1928 when they built the Ocatillo campsite near Chandler while working on the San Marcos-in-the-Desert Hotel drawings. And they spent the winter of 1934 there with the Taliesin Fellowship, making the Broadacre City models in the small town of Chandler, south of Phoenix.

In 1936-37 they went back with the intention of building a permanent winter home and studios there for themselves and for the Taliesin Fellowship. Mr. Wright "learned of a site 26 miles from Phoenix across the desert of the vast Paradise Valley. On up to a great mesa in the mountains. On the mesa just below McDowell Peak we stopped, turned and looked around. The top of the world! Magnificent—beyond words to describe! Splendid mystic desert vegetation."

By this time a turn in the economic tide had brought several new commissions into the office, the most important of these being Fallingwater, for Edgar J. Kaufmann, and the S. C. Johnson Wax Building, for Herbert F. Johnson. Other jobs for house designs were also on the boards at Taliesin. The construction of a new Taliesin, this time on the Arizona desert, now became feasible.

On November 12, 1937, in a letter written by Mrs. Wright to Mr. and Mrs. Mendel Glickman (an engineer who stayed at Taliesin for a period of time and worked on many of Mr. Wright's larger projects) she stated:

"We are all planning for a trip to Arizona in January. We will have sleeping bags and small tents. We will not build the camp. We are working on a trailer-kitchen, so we will be ever-moving in caravan for 3 months. There will be lots of hardships, but what fun! The Fellowship is very much excited over the coming adventure. As you know, any adventure under the leadership of Mr. Wright will be rich with all kinds of events...."

In 1938 Taliesin West, near Scottsdale, Arizona, was begun. The Fellowship established the pattern of spending part of the year at Taliesin in Wisconsin and the other part in Arizona. While the Fellowship was in Wisconsin in the summer a few people remained in Arizona to take care of the "Camp," as it was called for many years. The reverse took place during the winter months, with some of the students assigned to care for the Wisconsin property and tend the farm animals. Later on, Mrs. Wright's brother, Vladimir Lazovich, whom we affectionately called Uncle Vlado, and his wife, Aunt Sophie, remained at Taliesin West year round with the usual summer complement of apprentices to help in the work of maintenance and care of the buildings.

Once Taliesin West was established, the work schedule of the Fellowship increased at a steady pace. More and more architectural work, of vaster scope, came in. Hotels, civic centers, resorts, department stores, larger and larger building commissions were asked of Mr. Wright. During the forties, these large, imaginative projects were mostly left unbuilt because of the Second World War, but they remain in the vaults at Taliesin, an outstanding record of architectural genius, waiting for the day when they can be constructed. Residential work continued, always. Most large architectural firms, including that of Adler and Sullivan, Mr. Wright's early employers, refuse to design small private homes, since the cost of producing a set of plans is never covered by the commission charged. But from the beginning of his work, once his practice was established in Oak Park and Chicago, Mr. Wright accepted residential commissions. He adamantly believed that the construction of the moderate cost home for the American of limited income, conceived as a work of art as well as a solution to the clients' needs, was essential to the development of a culture in America. It was the larger commissions, however, that came in throughout Mr. Wright's career, that made possible this more modest residential work. ⌐

The innovative quality of Mr. Wright's creative life continued always to grow in his search for better solutions fitted to the needs of twentieth century man. New methods of construction and an ever broadening range of new materials demanded working drawings such as had never existed before in the world of architecture. The making of these drawings, carrying out Mr. Wright's sketches and details was, of course, the studio work of the Taliesin Fellowship. Soon added to this type of training was the work that had to be done in the field, where an apprentice who best understood the drawings and had helped to prepare them would go out and supervise construction.

The Second World War brought most architectural work to a halt. Because of the war effort building materials were scarce, some even nonexistent. Only one large project went forward to the working drawing stage, "Cloverleaf," a government housing project of quadruple houses designed for defense plant workers in Pittsfield, Massachusetts. But politics intervened when a Massachusetts Congressman asked: "Why has a Wisconsin architect been chosen to design a Massachusetts project?" The work was abruptly terminated.

The end of the war brought on a wave of new work, and at the same time a rush of apprentices from all over the world. From 1946 to 1959 the scope of Mr. Wright's creative work, both built and unbuilt, was staggering to behold. Sharing in all this work, witnessing its creation in original sketches, and participating in its working out was the Taliesin Fellowship. Firsthand we saw his ideas burst forth onto paper and become articulate in final drawings. When asked which of these buildings was his favorite, he always answered: "The next one."

By now the Fellowship was well known around the world and established as a significant entity. Built into the permanent life of Taliesin was a substantial core of men and women who made Taliesin their home and place of work and who were prepared to teach and assist in the training of new apprentices. As apprentices left, with a letter of recommendation by Mr. Wright, they set up their own practices wherever they chose, here in the United States and abroad. Taliesin was thus fulfilling its two-fold aim and purpose: to train architects who would go out and build fine and beautiful buildings; and to continue to develop a vibrant, ever-expanding training program.

When the Taliesin Fellowship opened in October of 1932, friends, relatives, clients, all predicted that such an enterprise would not survive six months. It has survived fifty years. It survived those lean and barren years of the Depression when money was scarce and architectural work even scarcer. It was then that Frank Lloyd Wright created his prophetic vision of the new American City, which he called Broadacre City, and later revised and published under the title *The Living City*. It survived the Second World War, although it was greatly depleted by the armed forces, leaving a work force that once again, as in the early thirties, had to turn to farming for its sustenance and livelihood. Nonetheless it was during this time that Mr. Wright designed the Guggenheim Museum and the Johnson Wax research tower.

It survived the sudden influx from Europe of a fashionable trend in architecture in the early fifties called "The International Style." Rich and influential American clients, conditioned by centuries of preferring anything European to anything American, rushed to the Bauhaus-trained architects. What they failed to realize, in paying homage to the International Style, was that it had all come to pass as a direct result of Mr. Wright's early work, mainly the Larkin Building of 1903 and the Unity Temple of 1905. Those works were admired abroad and carefully studied by European architects. But those architects misunderstood Mr. Wright's thesis, permitting science and technology to rule them, accepting the machine as their master. Mr. Wright's thesis was that the machine, as he termed it, "should be the tool in the hand of the artist." But the International Style posed no threat to him. International Style, he declared, was a misnomer: "it was neither International nor had any style." He regarded it as something that would rightfully die on the vine, and it has.

By far the most significant event that the Taliesin Fellowship had to survive was the death of Frank Lloyd Wright on April 9, 1959. His creative outpouring of new ideas had continued to grow right up to the moment of his death. In April of 1959 on the boards at Taliesin, and in construction around the nation, were the largest and now most famous of his later works. The Guggenheim Museum, the Beth Sholom Synagogue, and the Greek Orthodox Church in Milwaukee were then in construction. Working drawings were under way for the Marin County Civic and Government Center and for the Grady Gammage Memorial Auditorium. Many private residences were designed and under construction.

With more work on the drawing boards at Taliesin than there had ever been during Mr. Wright's lifetime, a group of apprentices, all personally trained by Mr. Wright, formed the architectural firm which we call the Taliesin Associated Architects. Mrs. Frank Lloyd Wright, as President of the firm, sent out the following letter:

"We wish to let you know that the work of The Frank Lloyd Wright Foundation will continue: I am President; William Wesley Peters, Vice President; and Eugene Masselink, Secretary-Treasurer. The Foundation is further ready and able to fulfill all existing contracts and to provide complete architectural services through the staff of the Taliesin Associated Architects.

Kindly address your requests for additional work of any nature to The
Frank Lloyd Wright Foundation, attention of William Wesley Peters.
With best wishes, sincerely yours,
Mrs. Frank Lloyd Wright, President
The Frank Lloyd Wright Foundation"

Today the educational aspect of the Taliesin Fellowship continues
under its new name, The Frank Lloyd Wright School of Architecture. The
architects of the firm teach the continuing influx of apprentices. Our
educational pattern in 1982 is much as it was in 1932: training by doing,
learning by experience, building buildings, maintaining them, working in
all day to day activities of life from the drafting room to the kitchen to the
gardens, and participating in the cultural activities at Taliesin.

Today, as the needs demand, our pattern of life changes—as Mr.
Wright would have wanted it to do. For him as for us, to be able to
change, to admit that one direction is finished and to launch courageous-
ly into another, is indicative of a youthful spirit. To retain this pervasive
quality of youthfulness in action, to accept change, based on sound principle, into the life of Taliesin, and for Taliesin to continue growing, pros-
pering, and developing these last twenty-two years is a living testimonial
to the genius of Frank Lloyd Wright.

October 1982 marks the half-century point in the life of the Taliesin
Fellowship. This volume commemorates that fiftieth anniversary by
presenting a selection of letters written by Frank Lloyd Wright to his apprentices, those men and women who worked by his side, and under his
supervision.

II

THE GROWTH OF AN IDEA

The earliest letters to applicants contain Mr. Wright's more personal explanation of the Taliesin Fellowship. These letters strive to make perfectly clear that education at Taliesin is not like anything the student may have seen or heard of before, and he cautions the incoming student neither to expect at Taliesin a standard college curriculum nor to come burdened with what he sometimes called "academic baggage."

Within a very few years the Fellowship prepared and sent out many fine architects. The ideas conceived in 1932 were developing deep roots and manifesting active results in architecture across the nation, proven by the work of these apprentices, now practicing architects. The Fellowship soon became widely known and it was no longer necessary for Mr. Wright to explain the training program of the Fellowship to applicants. Also, as there came an increase in architectural work, the demands required of him to answer letters from clients, contractors and builders around the country necessitated that letters to applicants and former apprentices be briefer.

Each morning Mr. Wright spent on the average of one and a half to two hours working on his correspondence. And whenever it was necessary to clarify the meaning of the Taliesin Fellowship and the Frank Lloyd Wright Foundation he still devoted much time and effort to make the significance of Taliesin clear. As the years progressed he was acutely aware of firmly establishing the permanence of Taliesin. He saw in this permanence the guarantee that his ideas and principles would persevere, would succeed him "for the next hundred years."

June 4, 1932

Miss Elizabeth Bauer
Vassar College, N.Y.

Elizabeth Bauer came as one of the first members of the Taliesin Fellowship, later married the Swiss architect Rudolph Mock, also one of the first apprentices. Now Elizabeth Kassler, she resides in Princeton, New Jersey.

My dear Elizabeth:

Since inquiries similar to yours are coming in perhaps this letter can be made to serve as answer for all alike.

1st: The Taliesin Fellowship is not to be a "school" in the ordinary sense of the term. It is really extension of the work in architecture as it has gone on for nearly twenty years here, at Taliesin, not only in the number of apprentices taken but gradually into the fields of the allied arts and eventually of allied industries as well.

This extension contemplates exactly 100 apprentices, about 40 girls and 60 boys and ten honor-apprentices whose relation to the 100 will be that of a senior leader competent in point of ability and character to be at the head of each group of ten. Each table in the dining room will seat a group of ten. (A system of interchange of the Fellows belonging to the various groups at table could be made to stimulate discussion and controversy at this social occasion.) These leaders will be selected from among the entire group by myself and the general leader who as yet is not determined upon. The group of artists described in the prospectus as at the center of the Fellowship work will all be competent and distinguished in their particular fields and I am taking my own time to decide upon them. I shall not announce them till next October.

Judging from the 36 or more applications already received, unsolicited, the general group will be made up of post-graduates from different universities in America and abroad. There will be no overseeing or restraints or tests applied to the workers except the preliminary one of fitness and character. We are not going to take any but good material judged by the same standards I have judged them by in taking them into Taliesin, hitherto.

Their previous training should have endowed them for the faculty of self-government, which system will prevail among the workers. So soon as an individual worker appears discontent, uninterested, incompetent or undesirable to the others he or she will promptly be dropped.

The Fellowship is primarily a band of volunteer workers interested in architecture as the center line or backbone of pretty much everything we call civilization and willing to co-operate on the basis of apprenticeship in getting the work which may be laid out for them done well and devising work for themselves.

Each will have three hours of work of some kind detailed to him or her by matron or farmsuperintendent (through the general manager of the physical plant, who is responsible for all work on the grounds and buildings) and necessary to the upkeep of the establishment every day, before entering the studio or laboratories. Each will have a modest, well appointed room of his or her own which, outside a general cleaning and changing of bed linen once every week each apprentice will be expected to keep in good order. The girls will be domiciled in a separate unit under their proper leaders and the boys in another unit grouped under their leaders.

There will be a general housemother or matron to look after the special needs of each worker. The members of the center of the ten groups will be in residence with their families.

There are fairly good country doctors within call in case of illness. (The general necessities of the students such as personal laundry etc. can be obtained in Spring Green connected with the School by car twice a day. All other services not obtainable in the village can be had in the state capitol of Madison connected with the school twice a week by the school bus at a cost to the students of fifty cents for the return trip.) No laundry will be done on the premises unless the students wish to do it themselves. Accommodations will be provided for this.

The full scope of the school will not be realized until the third year. Just how much of our programme we will begin with is yet uncertain except that the first year will be devoted to architecture and drawing. Everyone in the Fellowship must learn to draw, from nature and at the draughting board. Each student, of whatever predilection, will have a drawing table in the central draughting room under competent direction. A printing establishment will be joined to the drawing and model making, mold making and furniture making. There will also be music and rhythm and the general philosophy of the arts.

As for recreation--the country itself is very beautiful. There will be saddle horses to be rented for a small sum, motoring, driving, walking and the general exercise of field work and laboratory. Tennis. In the summer--swimming in the Wisconsin River and in Winter there are the hills and the small ponds for winter sports. There will be general meetings at the Chapel. The cinema two evenings each week and programs devised by the Fellowship itself. On Sunday the Fellowship will hold its own non-sectarian services at the Chapel. Many creative artists who have something to say will be heard, coming to the Fellowship as guests interested in our work.

We want to get away as much as possible from the stereotyped "institution" and in order to do so must not only choose our "Fellows" with considerable care but find in all a willing spirit and industrious co-operation in actual work. Ideas are to be directly connected with performance, as experience. No member of the Fellowship is other than a worker for his or her own growth as an individual in the development of the Fellowship as a whole. This is something which cannot be born readymade but must grow to be what the Fellows themselves are able to make it. So, in the best sense here is a chance to grow in individual power and breadth of individual resources.

The money paid in by the Fellows as well as their work will be used to support and continue the growth of the work--as will also such financial aid as may come our way from time to time as we demonstrate the Fellowship work and the Fellowship cause.

The Taliesin Fellowship will never be closed to growth except as to the number of Fellowships which will not change.

It is to begin on the centerline already established and none may say how far it will go or how quickly its work may expand. Much will depend upon the quality of the members of the Fellowship itself. The fee of 675 Dollars per year in such environment as we already have and in the comfortable circumstances we are setting up would be impossible on any other basis than each contributing his or her full share of co-operative work in the high spirit that is characteristic of any successful work in the arts.

I hope this will give Mrs. Bauer, your mother-- a general outline of the sort of a place and work you will be getting into, but she should, herself, come sometime and see the place and our work with her own eyes, for herself.

August 18, 1932
Miss Elizabeth Bauer

My dear Elizabeth:

Not hearing from you I imagined you had been unable to convince your parents and so wrote Miss Swan. I am enclosing a copy of her letter to me and of my reply to her.

We should be very glad indeed to save the place I had intended for you--that is to say I thought we could start you as one of the seven leading apprentices and depend upon you for some direct help in that capacity, finding the equivalent of a scholarship for you later on (or next year) among our financially competent friends if you were happy in the work here.

One hundred apprentices seems a crowd to me but I am still planning space for seventy which still seems a crowd. I wish I might reduce the number to thirty-five but then I could never take the more needy ones and they are the ones I most want. The tuition would have to be doubled and is small as it now stands--for the year's work. As you will see I offer more of myself at the beginning than I expect to give as the project develops. We are just now sending out the circular to applicants and sending one to you with the plan more definitely developed.

We shan't have the new buildings ready before October 20th but we can begin where and as we are at Taliesin. The date September 20th given Nathalie Swan was intended for those who want to come and help on the buildings, of whom there are many young men. You will have several girls for company, two Vassar girls, one from Bryn Mawr and Antioch, etc.

Lucienne Block also was headed this way but have not heard from her since she went to Detroit with Diego Rivera. It looks as though our fellowship would be about thirty per cent girls.

As I wrote you $300.00 now in making ready is worth to us twice the sum when we are ready, so you may send it in and consider yourself eligible and accepted for the coming year.

Yesterday we accepted the application of Miss Louise Dees-Porch of Reading, Mass.

Remember me to Catherine--very best to her.

September 22, 1932
Edgar A. Tafel
New York City

Believe we can manage a Fellowship for you if you pay all you can now--you may come now into temporary quarters if you like. My respects to Percival Goodman.

September 23, 1932
Manuel J. Sandoval
Chicago, Ill.

We can use good carpenters. So if you are alone and can come now, share accommodations, we may be able to make some arrangement later with workmen at Hillside.

October 1, 1932
Mr. W. F. Deknatel
Stamford, Conn.

My dear Deknatel:

I rather anticipated that if you didn't let me know, you were coming, and I've kept the room aside intended for you.

You may send us the regular preliminary fee ($270.--) at this time and we will expect you about October 20th.

Weather here is clear and sharp. We are in the North and sport clothes--the most comfortable wear.

My best to Mrs. Deknatel and we expect to like the little Deknatel.

April 3, 1933
Mr. Alden B. Dow
Midland, Michigan

My dear Alden Dow:

I have just returned from a lecture trip in the East and find your application for Fellowship.

I remember meeting you in Princeton and would be glad to have you at work here with us except that as a commuter from the outside--Ford or no Ford--I do not see you as an integral member of our group.

So I suggest that you take your room here as a regular and go to Madison whenever you were needed, or the spirit moved, and have Mrs. Dow share it with you week-ends or whenever she pleased. It is soon going to be nice to have an automobile objective in the country. And perhaps in time she, herself, might find a fellowship here, "educational" or at least helpful--with the university as collateral, although we are primarily interested in culture with an eye askance at Education as it is now practiced.

[It was soon discovered that to separate husband and wife during the husband's education at Taliesin became a dividing factor that seriously lessened his ability to learn and work. For this reason it was decided to accept married students on the condition that both join the Fellowship, pay tuition, and participate in the life at Taliesin.

From 1932 on a sense of absolute equality between men and women was established, and Fellowship wives learned to mix concrete, make architectural renderings, and participate in construction work even as the men learned to cook and bake and take care of the household.]

April 17,1933
Mr. A. M. Bush
Brooklyn, N.Y.

My dear Mr. Bush:

Mr. Jensen has handed me your letter.

The lad in question would have a better chance here as an individual than he would have in mass-production at Yale--all other things being equal. And they are not equal because the Fellowship is culture and Yale is merely "education" of a type that has manufactured helpless white-collarites by the thousand.

Taliesin would not supplement Alfred's cultural studies--but plant him in an atmosphere and in action where he would grow beyond anything otherwise possible to him and become independent in several directions where his living was concerned. If we feel that a boy needs special tutoring in certain technique--we will give it to him.

Concerning the money-matter. We are building our buildings with very little ready money in hand. Every dollar has to go a long way if we are to go on growing, so at the moment we badly need all we can get.

Could I suggest that you make the two preliminary payments and when the other falls due we would wait until your condition financially was easier? That we would do. Alfred's graduation at the high school is by no means important, I think. He would be better off to begin here next June and go on here with us. But I know the sentiment concerning "graduation". Perhaps he has it himself.

Kindly let us know your decision as early as possible.

April 23, 1933
Paul Frankl
New York City

Dear Paul:

I've not written for one reason because I feel deeply the responsibility I would take on toward you in taking your son--then came a week of real sickness--and your second letter.

As you know my feelings for you are deeply friendly. You have always been good to me in your fashion and your fashion has great charm. I suggest you bring the lad, as you have suggested, as early in the summer as you please. Let's see how he reacts to us and we to him?

We'll take him on as a regular Fellow for a year or more if you want us to take him when you feel it time for you to leave. We will enjoy having you with us and will look forward to your coming whenever you say when.

June 28, 1933
Mr. A. M. Bush
Brooklyn, N.Y.

My dear Mr. Bush:

Alfred arrived on schedule and seems like a promising youngster. He is our youngest apprentice. But when I saw him stripped to the waist with a stone hammer and chisel in his hand laying up a wall next morning, I saw too, that he is one of the sturdiest.

His room mate is Abe Dombar, one of our cleverest and nicest boys and I think they will hit it off well together.

As specified in the application for Fellowship, apprentices are to make the second installment of $450.-- when they enter the Fellowship.

If there is some misunderstanding concerning this feature kindly let us know as we have already anticipated the sum and spent it.

Money matters are an "emergency" here until next October--so forgive me for mentioning the matter so promptly.

My best to Alfred's parents.

July 3, 1933
Mr. Arthur Davison Ficke
Hillsdale, New York

My dear Arthur:

It is pleasant to hear from you. And I will be proud to have your son in our Fellowship. I imagine it is for such as your son the thing exists, and by way of Youth like the Youth I know as Arthur Davison Ficke--that the Fellowship will persist.

We will have several young married couples of good quality here so "Stan" will have joys and sorrows running parallel to his. But we have everything here, Arthur, except money--which we sorely need to get the instruments into our hands we must get completed to work with. The struggle is, at the moment, severe. But for this I would say, send Stan along and I would do my best to "initiate" him as I might on his own efforts. I hope this ability will come along as the Fellowship grows.

I am writing him that if he pays the regular tuition fee for himself as specified in the prospectus for the Fellowship that Miss Sally Stevens--(inasmuch as they will occupy a room together) may come by paying only the application fee of $200.00.

I have done this in the case of a clergyman's daughter who wanted to bring her husband with her to continue his development as an architect. This and one more consideration: it is that Stan's father agrees to spend at least one week here in residence every year lecturing daily to our boys and girls on whatever subject lies uppermost in him--at his convenience of course.

July 3, 1933
Mr. Stanhope B. Ficke
Annisquam, Mass.

My dear Stanley Ficke:

You are welcome as your father's son now, and doubtless soon, as yourself to join us at Taliesin and as Miss Sally Stevens will join you later--"for better or for worse."

The material consideration attached will be a tuition fee for yourself-- and the entrance fee for Mrs. Ficke,--a single room to you both for your private refuge. She to employ her time as you specify. But our aim here is just that "all round culture" you mention as her aim.

The Fellowship is a way of life as well as a way, and she as well as you would soon find your places where you needed them most.

Some strangers looking over our new buildings came across me on the Job (unrecognized, I suppose because of dirt and mortar) and asked: "What are they building here?"

"A refuge from the Universities." I said, "there is now no place to lay one's head,"--and walked off leaving them to figure it out.

We will abolish the month of trial in your case. But you may do in this matter as you please--and come when you are ready.

August 26, 1933
Mr. Eugene Masselink
Columbus, Ohio

Eugene Masselink joined the Fellowship in 1933. The next year he became Mr. Wright's personal secretary, and he later became the Secretary-Treasurer of the Frank Lloyd Wright Foundation.

Gene met Mr. Wright in 1932 when he arranged a lecture engagement at his fraternity in Michigan. Trained in painting, when he came to Taliesin he studied architecture directly with Mr. Wright. In the subsequent years he was commissioned to make many murals and paintings—often for the houses of Mr. Wright's clients.

Originally based on Mr. Wright's concept of rectilinear and geometric forms, the work Gene developed and carried forward in the art of abstraction was supremely creative. He helped to establish the Taliesin Press, designed our stationery, invitations, programs, and printed the "Taliesin Square Papers," a group of essays and addresses written by Mr. Wright.

He had a sonorous baritone voice, with a fine sense of musicianship to go with it, and he participated in the musical activities that were and still are so much a part of life at Taliesin.

Everyone who knew him thought the world of him; his humor was ever present, his wit a great delight. Following his untimely death in 1962, at the age of 51, Mrs. Wright wrote in her book, The Roots of Life: *"Dedicated to the memory of Eugene Masselink. There was no conflict between his faith and his life."*

My dear Masselink:

Ever since making your acquaintance I've waited to make a place for you here at the Fellowship and believe I can do it now.

Won't you write me of your circumstances and your plans?

October 27, 1933
The Senate of Tsing Hua College
Peking, China

Honored Sirs:

I submit for your distinguished consideration the fact that Mr. Yen Liang has showed much talent in his work here in the Taliesin Fellowship during the past year.

He is developing unusual abilities and I believe he has a brilliant future in architecture and the arts allied to it when, eventually, he returns to China if he can continue uninterrupted for at least another year.

His experience here is more directly related to the work he will be called upon to do when he returns than any college could allow him to perform. To continue that work with us next year ought to be of incalculable future benefit to his country.

In December of 1933, a new brochure was printed to describe the work of the Taliesin Fellowship after the first year had been completed. Some changes were in effect in the working out of details, but the basic learning principles remained constant.

Attached to this new brochure was the following list of the charter members of the Taliesin Fellowship, now called "Fellows."

Stephen Arneson St. Paul, Minn.
Margaret Asire Westerville, Ohio
Yvonne Bannelier Wood Paris, France
Betty Barnsdall Hollywood, Cal.
Elizabeth Bauer Princeton, N.J.
Paul Beidler Lehighton, Pa.
Christel Tessa Brey Chicago
William Bernoudy St. Louis, Mo.
Robert Bishop Swarthmore, Pa.
Ernest Brooks Tulsa, Oklahoma
Vissher Boyd Philadelphia, Pa.
Willets Burnham Winnetka, Ill.
Alfred Bush New York City
William Deknatel Paris, France
Geraldine Deknatel Paris, France
Abe Dombar Cincinnati, Ohio
Alden B. Dow Midland, Mich.
Vada Dow Midland, Mich.
James Drought Milwaukee, Wis.
George Dutton San Francisco
Ruth Dutton San Francisco
Charles Edman Jr. Monte Vista, Colorado
A. C. Van Elston Muscoda, Wis.
Stanhope B. Ficke Davenport, Iowa
Sally S. Ficke Cambridge, Mass.
William Beye Fyfe Oak Park, Ill.
Mendel Glickman Milwaukee, Wis.
Phillip Holliday Fairmount, Ind.
John H. Howe Evanston, Ill.
Karl E. Jensen Copenhagen
Else Klumb Cologne
Michael Kostanecki Krakow, Poland
Frederick Langhorst Elgin, Ill.
John Lautner Marquette, Mich.
Yen Liang Peking, China
Charles Grey Martin Bedford, Ia.
Eugene Masselink Grand Rapids
Rudolph Mock Zurich, Switzerland
Chandler Montgomery Chicago

Robert Mosher Bay City, Michigan
Takehiko Okami Tokyo
Wm. Wesley Peters Evansville, Ind.
Louise Dees Porch Reading, Mass.
Samuel Ratensky Brooklyn, N.Y.
Nicholas Ray La Crosse, Wis.
Manuel Sandoval Nicaragua
Irving Shaw Minneapolis
Mary Roberts Marquette, Mich.
Henry Schubart New York City
Lewis Stevens Milwaukee
Edgar Tafel New York City
Elizabeth Weber Wilmette
Svetlana Wright Taliesin
Thomas Wigle Detroit
Harry Yardley Philadelphia

This first group of Fellows produced many people who were to become the nucleus of the Taliesin Fellowship, and who would subsequently be responsible for the carrying on of Taliesin. Two outstanding members on this list were Eugene Masselink and William Wesley Peters.

Wes came to Taliesin in the fall of 1932 and has worked at Taliesin to this day, now as Vice-President of The Frank Lloyd Wright Foundation. Trained as an engineer at M.I.T., he is also a very sensitive designer and architect. From 1932 to 1959, he engineered and supervised many of the larger commissions, including Johnson Wax, Florida Southern College, and the Guggenheim Museum.

Wes married Mrs. Wright's oldest daugther, Svetlana. He developed a keen interest in farming, and purchased the farm house that Mr. Wright had lived in when, as a boy, he was sent each summer by his mother to work on his Uncle James' farm in the ancestral Lloyd Jones valley. Mr. Wright described Wes and his support of Taliesin in his Autobiography *in a segment called Aldebaran, the name that Wes gave to his farm:*

"Our son-in-law bought the ground--named it Aldebaran (the follower), and Taliesin soon after jumped to the control of about one thousand acres with about three miles of waterfront. The naming of the place shows the spirit of the lad: a genuine apprentice. His ambitions were not cheap: individuality strong. He didn't need to worry about that. He was glad and proud to stand by and contribute his strength to Taliesin and Taliesin appreciated him, believed in him as much as he believed in Taliesin. Here was apprenticeship in flower. Wes planned his house on that nearby hill--a well-conceived house for his young wife, who gave him a young son they named Brandoch, a name which puts it up to the boy to be at least a hero.

"Taliesin had a daughter, a son and a grandson. Taliesin has other faithful competent sons--an asset to Fellowship, but none with more strength, energy and loyalty than the young man Olgivanna and I drove away years ago on the unkind assumption that he was stealing a daughter. Well, Svetlana, the daughter, is now somebody in her own right.

"Here in the Wisconsin Hills, Aldebaran is Taliesin's first real extension--collateral human growth. But inside Taliesin Wes is a young leader and the charming lively Svetlana--both have a large share in cultivating the life of the Fellowship. Svetlana has an innate sense of music. Wes is so interested in farming that I can scarcely get Architecture out of him or into him anymore. But it is there and makes, I guess, a Taliesin showpiece.

"Wes (then ten years at Taliesin) is a right bower, example of What-Taliesin-Can-Do-for-a-Young-Apprentice (his wife thrown in) and, what a young apprentice can do for Taliesin."

In September of 1946, Svetlana and her youngest son, Daniel, were killed in a tragic automobile accident on the road to Spring Green. Writing to Herbert Johnson of Johnson Wax Company Mr. Wright said:

October 10, 1946

Dear Hib:

Thank you and Irene for your kind thought for us in deep trouble. The wound is very deep. Poor Wes!

Lovely Svetlana was so important to our life here that we are numb for the time being. Olgivanna takes it very hard.

Seems as though I've had more than my share of grief--but my joy in life has been great Hib--

Perhaps one has to pay for the one with the other?

September 11, 1934
Alden Dow
Midland, Michigan

My dear Alden:

I didn't think it would be so many months before I would write acknowledging the check you sent to help keep fine oak trees from walking out of the neighborhood. I planked it down on the contract I had made to keep 709 logs where they lay on the ground about a mile away. They are lying there yet because I haven't yet completed the payment and had no saw mill. We now have a saw mill and I expect to have the logs moved down and sawed while we are in the desert this winter.

Plans for that "hegira"--I am fond of them--are under way and we are busy on the monograph TALIESIN at the moment.

I've heard gossip concerning your doings up there as you have heard gossip concerning ours down here and hope all goes well. If we all keep well that is best of all, because our efforts are dated so far ahead that they often seem unimportant. So far as Olgivanna, Iovanna and myself are concerned we've had an active happy summer. When we look around we see what we still haven't done. But others coming in see what we have done and they are usually amazed.

Deck and Gerry, for instance, with whom we spent a most pleasant and gratifying time.

We have had few genuine fellowships as yet. I mean by that the devotion to the ideal we had in mind here that would exclude outside interest and concentrate on the work here as a major interest. Of course I have yet "chosen" no one in that connection. Nearly everyone showing up here is tied back or up or down somehow into the system and comes to take out what he can take away as soon as he can. Nevertheless the spirit here has been good and within their limitations the boys and girls have done their damndest best. I have no reason to complain and much to thank them for as I do, and go on cheerfully coaching competitors instead of cooperators. But this winter I am going to take it easier with a group of some fifteen I will take with me to the grand scale of Arizona. A complete change.

We will probably go in with Dr. Chandler until we get our own camp built. I have wished from time to time we had a print of the moving pictures you made here. Perhaps it is only fair that a print for our own use should be our natural share in the circumstances. We were the subject you know. You are no doubt too "busy" (I think that is the word) to have one made for us so won't you allow us to have one made? It might help our work here to have it.

We have about the same bunch of "human nature" now as when you were here--so you may imagine what goes on. Five new members appear this fall--Stamo Papadaki the Greek architect among them. And we hope to hear from the Soviet concerning three scholarships. We are to have one from Stanley Marcus in Texas and a young girl comes from Dublin University and one from Cambridge. I want Yen to bring back a young Chinese wife and settle here if the spirit moves him (the first invitation to join the central corps) and from Japan I expect a young couple--in January.

The Fellowship as I conceive it now is still an open matter with the wisdom gained from two years experience with such material as happened--go lucky--to it to our credit and also some little of it--go unlucky--to our discredit--be it said.

We often speak of you and Vada and hope "the little hell of your own" keeps hot enough to suit you. With warm regards to you both from we, us and company--

September 21, 1934
Donald Thompson
Cleveland, Ohio

My dear Donald Thompson:

This is coming along at a tardy rate. But it is to say that if you care to join us now, with your wife, we will be glad to give you the equivalent of a scholarship. The place needs someone with knowledge of motors and machinery to keep it going and you could in this respect as well as in helping to plan our installations be valuable to our work here.

We are very much "in the making" yet. Falling down and getting up again but each time we get up a little stronger which is a good sign for the future. I suspect this pioneering against the current or across the grain is good for humans.

Let me know how you are situated--

October 16, 1934

My dear Donald Thompson:

If I did not believe you would gain something of value while you helped us put the young Fellowship on a workable basis I wouldn't have written to you. If I did not believe you would both take hold of the practical side of things here with a will and purpose to do all you can do to help in every way you can I wouldn't write now. But I believe in both these beliefs.

Mrs. Thompson can be a great help to Mrs. Wright who is single hand-ed now in our quarters and Mrs. Wright can be a great help to Mrs. Thompson. As you describe her it seems to me she would not be content to be idle and the more responsibility she took the more she would feel at home.

Taliesin is a homelike place. There is nothing of the institution. No formality. Not enough, probably. You and Mrs. Thompson are coming as pace makers to help keep up morals and keep things moving. We have a number of sons and daughters of the rich that need good exemplars.

I wish we might have had your engineering help earlier in getting our heating system installed. You might have had a good scheme. But it is going in now.

But many things remain to be done to put our mechanical appliances-light--water and transportation--as well as our shop machinery into better effect.

Too much of our time goes into running after things to fix them up so we can fix them again--etc. etc.

But there is nothing "stock" in the programme. We will make adjustments when we get together that are agreeable all around.

We will look for you preferably Saturday, November tenth to share in our weekend occasions at home and at the Playhouse.

We will be ready for you Saturday evening for dinner. We are one hour ahead of Standard time in our region and dine at seven. That would be at six standard.

My best to you both--

[The weekend occasion mentioned above refers to the tradition of cinema and musical concerts established in 1932 and continuing to this day. Of all the arts related to the great Mother Art of Architecture, music was the one that Mr. Wright considered to be the closest. Fine music too possesses a sense of structure, in its sounds as well as its rhythms. On Saturday evenings a formal dinner was held in the theater (the Hillside gymnasium converted into a playhouse) and followed by a film. Sunday evenings took place in the living room at Taliesin,--again a formal dinner, but this time followed by a concert. A chorus of Fellowship members sang and there were various instrumental groups including a chamber ensemble and later a recorder choir.]

By the end of 1936, the construction of Fallingwater was under way and Johnson Wax Company was in the working drawing stage. Several smaller houses were on the boards at Taliesin, and there were prospects of further commissions. After a long period of no architectural work, the studio was now full to capacity.

September 3, 1936
Fred Langhorst
Seattle, Washington

My dear Fred:

It is a shame that you had no word from me to express my appreciation of your Christmas card and your thought in it. It was good.

I think of you often and hope you are gaining wisdom with experience.

Taliesin seems to be getting the breaks at last.

If you come East, come up.

September 3, 1936
William A. Bernoudy
St. Louis, Mo.

My dear Billy:

Your letter amused me as it pleased me. Amused me that you should
see now what I thought you were seeing all the time.

Taliesin seems to be getting a chance now. Too bad you are outside
looking in and not inside looking out.

January 8, 1942

To Whom It May Concern:

William A. Bernoudy was an apprentice in the Taliesin Fellowship
under my direction from October 1932 to October 1935 and gave an excellent account of himself in every way.

September 25, 1936
Kevin Lynch
New Haven, Conn.

*This letter to apprentice Kevin Lynch includes a valuable statement.
No longer are the applicants accepted by mail; they must now come for*

a personal interview with Mr. Wright before he decides to let them enter.

My dear Kevin Lynch:

Answering your questions about Fellowship at Taliesin--
1. Your stay at Yale could be no possible help to your work at Taliesin.
2. Your lack of ability to draw is soon rectified.
3. We have no courses nor any curriculum at Taliesin. Only performance under my direction and alongside other apprentices.
4. No engineering courses will help you here except as they are not anterior but posterior to experience in learning the nature of the thing to which they apply. The sense of the whole and its philosophy first. Technique first is the cart before the horse.
5. Theory and practice are one at Taliesin.
6. City planning is natural feature of our work at Taliesin (Broadacre City).
7. The best time for an architect in embryo to join the Fellowship is before any time is wasted along conventional educational lines in architecture or engineering.

We should want to see you and talk with you personally and have you see us before we agree to take you into Fellowship. And you would be welcome at any time for that interview.

On a trip to Arizona in November and December of 1937, Mr. and Mrs. Wright finally decided upon the site of land that they wished to purchase, and Mr. Wright sent this telegram to Gene Masselink in Wisconsin:
"WEATHER WARM. BEAUTIFUL SITE IN HAND. COME JOKAKE INN SOON YOU ARE READY. BRING SHOVELS, RAKES, HOES, AND ALSO HOSE. EIGHTEEN DRAFTING BOARDS AND TOOLS. WHEELBARROW, CONCRETE MIXER, SMALL KOHLER (ELECTRICAL PLANT) AND WIRE. MELODEON, OIL STOVES FOR COOKING AND HEATING. WATER HEATER, VIOLA, CELLO, RUGS NOT IN USE AND WHATEVER ELSE WE NEED."
Soon the Fellowship arrived on the desert. Temporary camping quarters were set up and the construction of Taliesin West began. First came the large drafting room, which served also as dining room, music room, and assembly room until the rest of the buildings were completed. There was no water, no electricity, no heating, no plumbing. It was completely a life of camping out, rugged, sometimes difficult, primitive in many aspects—but a great venture was under way.
Only later was a well shaft driven into the Mesa depths for water and a diesel plant installed to supply electricity. An apprentice court was built

to house the nine senior members, while the other apprentices lived, as the students do today, in tents, often developed into elaborate structures of imaginative beauty.

In his Autobiography Mr. Wright summed up Taliesin West as follows:

"The Arizona camp is something one can't describe, just doesn't care to talk much about. Something sacred in respect to excellence....

"Our new desert camp belonged to the Arizona desert as though it had stood there during creation. And also built into Taliesin West is the best in strong young lives of about thirty-five young men and women during their winter seasons for about seven years. Some local labor went in too, but not much. The constant supervision of an architect--myself, Olgivanna inspiring and working with us all, working as hard as I--all living a full life..."

And in a letter to Fowler McCormick, son of Harold McCormick of International Harvester, he later wrote:

March 31, 1949

Dear Fowler:

Replying to your kind note...

You are perfectly right in feeling the primitive in Taliesin West. In the ancient days of the race men were close to nature as a child to its mother. They were naturally inspired and taught by her forms. They had no choice.

Sophistication came with Science and what we call education to wean or warp them away from the simplicity of that childhood.

Now, Mankind, as degeneracy looms, needs the refreshment afforded by a conscious return to the verities of being--returning to Nature not only in that early obvious sense but with more prophetic understanding and appreciation.

Well, Fowler—Taliesin West is modeled with that higher understanding--deeper than the simplicity of the barbarian, not copying his forms but drinking understanding from the springs from which he drank unconsciously. The result is not imitation but inspiration from the same source--now enlightened and furnished in action with more ample means to create symphony where before only the natural response of the child existed.

Modern art feels the need of the inner strength that comes from this eternal inspiration. But, being weak falls into imitation instead of creation. Of this imitation Taliesin is not guilty.

Taliesin West is as original as the Maya but far beyond it. More natural to environment and our life in that desert than the barbarians could have been in his time and consciously proud of it in this time.

But we shouldn't be too proud? Or we fall.

Studio at Taliesin 1937

Top row, left to right: Carey Carraway, John Lautner, John Howe, Eugene Masselink, Blaine Drake, Ellis Jacobs, E. Brookins, Herbert Fritz, Burton Goodrich, Edgar Tafel. Bottom row, left to right: Benjamin Dombar, Kevin Lynch, James Thomson, Wesley Peters, Robert Mosher.

Taliesin North early winter

Hillside (Hillside Home School Building, 1902, remodeled 1932, 1952)

Constructing Taliesin West

Taliesin West   1938

Taliesin West   1958

Taliesin West against the McDowell Mountains   1956

Now that the Taliesin Fellowship had expanded to fifty-five members and had two facilities at its disposal, Taliesin for summer living, and Taliesin West for the winter, this new brochure was composed and stayed in use until Mr. Wright's death in 1959.

THE TALIESIN FELLOWSHIP

THE TALIESIN FELLOWSHIP OF THE FRANK LLOYD WRIGHT FOUN-DATION INCLUDES APPRENTICESHIPS FOR ABOUT FIFTY FIVE YOUNG MEN AND WOMEN IN THE PHILOSOPHY AND PRACTICE OF ORGANIC ARCHITECTURE AND THE WAY OF LIFE--DEMOCRACY--OF WHICH IT IS CHARACTERISTIC. APPRENTICES PREPARE PLANS, DETAILS, AND MODELS FOR BUILDING CON-STRUCTION, WORK UPON CONSTRUCTION GOING ON THROUGHOUT THE YEAR, SHARE IN THE TILLING OF TALIESIN FARM FIELDS AND GARDENS AND PERFORM SATISFACTORILY THE DAILY UPKEEP NECESSARY FOR THEIR OWN LIFE AT TALIESIN. ACTION IN MANY CHANGING FIELDS IS ESSENTIAL TO TALIESIN EXPERIENCE.

For many years past a small freely changing group of about fify five young men and women--volunteers from our own and many foreign countries--have formed a faithful group of apprentices to the ideals and precepts of the Taliesin Fellowship conceived and formulated by Mr. and Mrs. Frank Lloyd Wright. Taliesin nourishes sincerity of character and pur-pose in the novice. In every action experience stimulates the growth of whatever talent an apprentice may possess.

For six summer months of each year--May to November--we are situated on the Midwest acreage at Taliesin where southern Wisconsin is most lovable. We are continually expanding and maintaining the buildings originally built in 1903 and developing the rural landscape ac-cording to the concepts of decentralization indicated by Broadacre City. We have a spacious draughting room and studios for painting and sculpture as well as workshops for pottery, weaving, glass-mosiac and other media. A little playhouse is designed for our own entertainment and adequate kitchen and dining facilities and living accommodations are provided.

For the winter months--November to May--we leave Wisconsin, tak-ing our work along in order to keep on working out of doors. We go to the extensive desert camp and workshops created by ourselves on the great Maricopa Mesa, twenty six miles northeast of Phoenix, Arizona. There, with all the facilities provided at Taliesin in Wisconsin, we con-tinue the work-program of the Fellowship without change.

All apprentices are expected to fulfill the tasks assigned to them in the studios, construction and maintenance. Participation in the chorus and chamber ensemble as well as in the rhythmic correlation-study of the dance is encouraged by the leaders of the Fellowship but is not obligatory.

The way of life at Taliesin is intended to be spontaneous experience, lived in atmosphere as natural and true to organic architecture as we can make it.

Under the direct guidance and inspiration of Mr. and Mrs. Wright, all apprentices are the working comrades of a faculty of nine senior members of the staff-- men and women who have been "seeing it through" for a long time and have gained the knowledge of getting the basic principles of Organic Architecture into actual practice. No apprentice can well avoid the implications of such thinking as he sees growing up around him at work in the Fellowship at Taliesin. Nor can he get away from the ultimate effects of such basic association so long as he lives.

To begin with, each novice deposits the yearly fee needed to help pay the actual cost of his "upkeep". The Foundation's stake in him is his Spirit and what work he is able to do. Spirit counts most at Taliesin. Nor are we much interested in getting anyone ready to earn money as of the present--architectural brokerage or wagery being what it is. The damage such premature technical preparation has done to the Cause of Architecture is now all too evident. We regard technical engineering not as preparation but as consequent to Architecture. An engineer is a rudimentary undeveloped architect.

At this time in our national life if we mean to be a democracy, the architect must himself be capable, because of actual experience, of going through from design to the completed building including furnishings and landscape.

Taliesin aims to produce a master builder thoroughly developed as a man and so able to take his place in the broad scheme of things in America on a basis liberal and genuinely significant of the organic ideal to whomever would build any building. To make young men and women ready for such active responsibility is the opportunity we seek to keep open to them here.

If someday Democracy is going to build for itself we must look to the individual as master in all aspects of any building he undertakes. Each building, however small, may mean mastership or failure. Big buildings are built only as capacity to build the small one is well assured.

Young people are at Taliesin because they love architecture and believe in Organic Architecture. We at Taliesin believe Democracy will, with the right encouragement, work well if allowed to do so.

Taliesin. Spring Green. Wisconsin. May to November
Taliesin West. Scottsdale. Arizona. November to May

FRANK LLOYD WRIGHT
Taliesin   Spring Green   Wisconsin

March 29, 1938
Mr. Robert Carroll May
Ann Arbor, Michigan

Dear Robert:

We will be at Taliesin about May 20th so come along then and we will be glad to receive you and will break you in.

June 13, 1938
Bob May

Dear Bob:

Meantime if you haven't spent your money or changed your mind, or changed your money and spent your mind, we'll be seeing you.

October 11, 1938
Consul General
Warsaw, Poland

Marya Lilien first came to the Fellowship in 1936 from Poland where she was born and educated. She returned to Warsaw to practice architecture, but Hitler's armies forced her to once again leave Poland. Her safe return to the U.S. was arranged through the help of a client, Otto Mallery of Sun Top Homes, who was involved with the Immigration Services.

Dear Sir:

Marya Lilien, architect, residing in Poland, desires to return to the United States on a permanent visa to continue her work as apprentice in the Taliesin Fellowship under my direction.

I will grant to Miss Lilien an extension of the scholarship she has had in the Taliesin Fellowship which will completely take care of her lodging, food, and tuition expenses for three years and I will guarantee she will not become a public charge.

I hope you will do whatever you can to facilitate her departure for America as soon as possible.

November 28, 1938
F. Bruce Maiden
Oakland, California

My dear Mr. Maiden:

Glad Son is getting better. Have him join us in Arizona--Phoenix--
December 15th. Let him advise us exactly when he will arrive in Phoenix
and we will arrange to meet him. Our address in Arizona is Scottsdale.

December 29, 1941

My dear Howard Ten Brink:

I've been about almost continually across the country coast to coast
and your letter has been neglected. I think I see in yourself and your lady
a good prospect for us as I see in us a good prospect for you. If you pay
what you can when you come and undertake to do your best with the
balance--that part of the affair would be all right with us.

We need fellows with your experience and we need a cellist for our
quartette among other pressing needs.

Let us know when you will arrive.

August 14, 1942
Mr. David T. Henken
Sunnyside, New York

My dear David Henken:

We have your application duly filled out in proper order and shall be
glad to see you when you arrive on October first. Your wife will be
welcome, too, whenever she comes.

Bring with you warm outdoor sport and work clothing as well as light
weight clothing--"coveralls". Your good clothes will serve for the occasions when the Fellowship "dresses up" Saturday and Sunday evenings
and other occasions. Strictly formal clothes are no essential. Bring your
own bedding: sheets, blankets, etc., and if you happen to have sleeping
bags bring them with you as you will find them useful on excursions.
Bring whatever drawing materials you have and what books and records
you wish. You will be given a room which you can suitably furnish

yourselves. You will need little furniture (the essentials--bed springs and mattress, etc., are all here).

We shall expect Mrs. Henken, as well as yourself, to enter into the work-life of the Fellowship--keeping up her share of the daily chores which she will like to do, I am sure. Work in all branches of maintenance-sharing, serving at meals, cooking in turn, etc., etc. The present Fellows alternate in these services so none have more than one week in one month--each takes a week at this maintenance job. We are looking forward to seeing you and Mrs. Henken in our Fellowship family circle. I am sure you will both contribute much to our daily life.

May 5, 1943
Delbert Larson
Sandy, Utah

My dear Delbert Larson:

At Taliesin we have considered your case. And believing you to be a good worker and very much in earnest we have decided to have you come on the terms you propose. Kindly fill out the enclosed application blank and send on.

Our work this summer is pretty largely agriculture and building, gardening and the maintenance of the Fellowship itself. You will be expected to take a hand in all this. Let us know when you will arrive.

August 4, 1944
Russ Leavenworth
Camp Campbell, Kentucky

Dear Russ Leavenworth:

Better to enter the Fellowship with no eye on a degree which is, after all, a scrap of paper.

No academic preparation is necessary to enter Taliesin.

We require good correlation, character and a love of Architecture and such. I believe we would be happy to use you.

Blanks (to fill out) enclosed.

There had been—in the initial years—a few apprentices from European and Asiatic nations, but with peace somewhat restored around the globe in the years following 1945, Taliesin began to see an influx of apprentices from all parts of the world. It pleased Mr. Wright to see the interest in his work and the education at Taliesin spread among young people around the world, and he accepted these students from foreign countries without the customary interview beforehand. If they could manage the voyage to the United States, he often gave them scholarships for their education at Taliesin. With students now free of the war effort, the enrollment of Americans increased as well.

February 25, 1946
Paolo Soleri
Torino, Italy

My dear Soleri:

If you can get here we will give you a fair trial in working your way through without tuition fee--

April 13, 1946
Mahmoud Omar
c/o Egyptian Education Office
Washington, D.C.

Dear Omar:

Strikes me the "Dept." is parsimonious. Why don't you say to them you would like so much to see our Arizona.
I think they would come across. We should like to start you in here. Have wired the Dept. to that effect.

August 21, 1946

My dear Gordon [Lee]:

Taliesin has reason to respect you and would be pleased to welcome you back again.
But Gordon there is this to consider--there are already six or seven boys here on the G.I. Bill of Rights as well as a number of C.O.s. You

would agree with neither? Are you sufficiently liberal in your attitude to be happy with them?

Concerning "wages"...the Foundation doesn't pay them. By the Foundation I mean myself as ourselves and ourselves as myself adding up to a cultural endeavor exempt from income taxes, etc., just like any university. Money is not of first importance except when there.

So what we would like to do and do is to set aside a stipend for the boys who cast in their lot here at Taliesin. The stipend is a dollar a day plus their living--all except clothing and doctor's and dentist's bills. Soon we may take over the matter of the doctor and the dentist.

Gene and I did a little figuring not so long ago and arrived at the conclusion that after a conservative valuation of our plant each "apprentice" costs us about $3,800.00 per year without adding to that sum what we pay them.

The Foundation owns my services and the ownership brings about seventy five thousand dollars a year with which we support ourselves and build for growth and experience. I keep nothing for myself and family but a living.

It is all fun. Fun for me and mine and increased capacity to build. That is all.

We are now over-full: sixty five. Too large! But we plan to send boys who work on plans out to build the buildings and there they will have salaries paid by the clients commensurate with the "cash and carry" system in which they build. You would quite likely be able to take such responsibility soon and go out--which would assuage the money matter to your satisfaction perhaps. We need builders and intend to make them. If they want to call themselves architects that is their affair? You would be welcome on the plan mentioned above.

Glad to know Fred has a good ski view where he sits and works and wish him well. He is better off where he is than he would be here.

September 21, 1946

Dear Steve [Oyakawa]:

Mrs. Wright and I as well as the Fellowship were pleased to hear again from you.

At Taliesin we are all busy and well--more work and more "Fellows" than ever. We miss you in our "International Set"--some eleven nations represented now. A real U.N.O.

Good Luck--

February 13, 1947
E. P. Abeywardene
Ceylon House, Bombay

Dear Mr. Abeywardene:

The conditions of Fellowship at Taliesin are enclosed. If you can comply--you would be welcome to join us.

March 24, 1947
Henry J. Allen
Wichita, Kansas

Dear Henry:

We'll be happy to meet John Hickman and hope he will work into the Fellowship (although it is already overcrowded)--anything you suggest, we do.
And here's faithful affection from...

[Henry J. Allen had a house designed by Frank Lloyd Wright in 1917, at the time he was Governor of Kansas. Whenever the Fellowship traveled in caravan between Taliesin and Taliesin West, the Allens always graciously invited them in.]

Arata Endo and Aisaku Hayashi were two of Mr. Wright's friends from the time he worked on the Imperial Hotel--1913 to 1922. Endo was his devoted right hand man in the design and construction of the building; Hayashi was the general manager of the Hotel. At the end of World War II Mr. Wright was deeply concerned for them, and wrote to General MacArthur to try and help them. Eventually the sons of these two friends would come to Taliesin as apprentices. Raku Endo now practices in Japan and occasionally returns to Taliesin to pay his respects to his "American family."

April 25, 1947
General Douglas MacArthur
United States Army Headquarters
Tokyo, Japan

Dear General:

Forgive me this cutting of red tape to appeal to you to enable me to help two faithful Japanese friends and cause the enclosed check to be given to Arata Endo, my faithful assistant in the building of the Imperial Hotel, Tokyo. Endo-san may be reached through the doctor of the Tokyo Imperial Univesity. If he and his family could be transferred to me at Spring Green, Wisconsin I would guarantee his independence (financially) of any government aid. His address is as follows: No. 4002, 8-chome, Shiina-machi, Toshima-ku, Tokyo.

And the manager of the Imperial Hotel at the time I built it was Aisaku Hayashi. I enclose a similar amount to help him. His address is 1410 Hase, Kamakura, Japan. If Hayashi-san and his wife could be sent to Spring Green I should be glad to guarantee his independence of government aid. If one of your secretaries will advise me how this could be accomplished--if both these Japanese are willing--I should appreciate it more than I can ever say. I feel greatly indebted to them for their immense loyalty.

And, General, may I commend your humanity toward the conquered. It is a bright spot in a dark picture.

June 2, 1952
Mr. Shichiro Hayashi
Kamakura, Japan

Dear Mr. Hayashi:

This letter is to advise you that The Frank Lloyd Wright Foundation has agreed to give you training in Organic Architecture for the period of one year.

We shall arrange finance for your passage to and from this country and your living expenses while here.

August 31, 1952

Dear Raku [Endo]:

If you can manage to get here, you will be a very welcome apprentice at Taliesin because of the love I bore your good father--my samurai. Eventually, I am sure, for your own sake.

My best regards to your mother--

April 26, 1947
George Thomson
Ithaca, New York

Dear George:

Notwithstanding your final conclusion to come to Taliesin, upon reading your letter I feel that it would be a mistake for us to take you in with us. I was glad, however, to hear from Dees Porch and Betty Weber again--long ago when Taliesin's diapers were out on the line they spent a brief time with us....
We are badly oversize at present--some 21 nations are represented among us. But we teach nothing. This is not a school. We are a strongly individual work. And so as a fountain head we are not for all and sundry. Taliesin is an experience that so far as I know has hurt no one yet--except us maybe.

May 7, 1947
Bruno Morassutti
Padua, Italy

My dear Morassutti:

Kindly send us some drawings of yours and a little more concerning yourself and your friend. We might make a place for you.
Do you know Bruno Zevi (Associazione Per l'Architettura Organica, Roma, via Quattro Fontane, Palazzo del Drago).

June 12, 1947

To whom it may concern:

Tore Erlingsonn Bjornstad [Norway] has been accepted as an apprentice in the Taliesin Fellowship under my direction starting immediately.

June 16, 1947

To the Italian Consul:

Paolo Soleri of Torino Italy is enrolled as apprentice in architecture with The Frank Lloyd Wright Foundation. He is doing excellent work and I wish him to continue his study for as long a time as it will be possible for him to do so.

I hope you will be able to help him in whatever is necessary to extend his stay in this country.

July 14, 1949

Ling Po, whose real name is Chow Yi-Hsien, was born in China and first came to Taliesin in 1946. He later returned to China, then wrote to Mr. Wright to ask if he could come back to Taliesin and bring his mother with him. (Otherwise she would be left alone in a changing China as it advanced toward communism.) Mr. Wright agreed. It was Mr. Wright who "christened" him Ling Po, a name which he still carries.

Ling is a staff member with a fine sense of style both in design and dance-drama.

Dear Ling:

I shall be happy to have you back in the Fellowship and expect you to stay until I say "go." Your mother will be welcome but we will have to provide for her within the accommodations of the Fellowship as we may--and expect her to be a good member according to her abilities. She will soon speak enough English.

Remember me to your sister, and if you can bring along a good gardener--there is a life position for him at Taliesin.

The copying of the Ku Hung Ming was a remarkable act.

On gratitude--a great contribution. Who wrote it?

May 25, 1948

To whom it may concern:

Calvin L. Stempel *[Panama]* has been accepted as apprentice in Architecture under my direction in The Frank Lloyd Wright Foundation.

His apprenticeship begins as soon as he is free to come into the country and we hope the necessary papers will be granted to him without delay.

June 11, 1948

To whom it may concern:

Gudmund Marteinson *[Iceland]* is an apprentice in Architecture under my direction in the Taliesin Fellowship.

October 16, 1948
Russi B. J. Patell
Bombay, India

My dear Russi Patell:

If you can reach us on your own steam we will put you to work. You seem like our kind of young man--

December 1, 1948
Pandit Jawaharlal Nehru
Prime Minister
New Delhi, India

My dear Pandit Nehru:

The leader of this architectural Fellowship is one of your great admirers.

Mansinhji M. Rana came to us to join the Taliesin Fellowship as an apprentice in Architecture under my direction in March 1946. He had a private loan scholarship from the Maharaja of Porbandar which was promised to him for at least three years. There was no written agreement, however, and under the changed circumstances of Free India for some reason the scholarship has been stopped.

Mansinhji is doing excellent work with us here in the Fellowship and I believe will prove a valuable asset to his country as an architect if he can continue his work with us for at least another three years.

My client, Gautam Sarabhai of Amedabad for whom we are building a department store and Mr. U. Meherally both of whom have visited us at Taliesin can tell you in detail about the work we are doing with young architects from all over the world.

What may be done about obtaining a scholarship for Mansinhji for several years? The tuition is $1,100.00 per year and he would need about $15.00 per month for his personal expenses. I believe he has no means of his own whatever and the unexpected withdrawal of the Maharaja's support leaves him in an embarrassing position--

March 14, 1949
Mr. Arthur E. Pfeiffer
Framingham Centre, Mass.

My dear Mr. Pfeiffer:

Thank you. I guess your son is in the right place for a budding genius--

September 25, 1950
DESMOND DALTON
c/o IRISH CONSULATE GENERAL
N.Y.C.

DEAR DALTON:

SO FAR AS TALIESIN IS CONCERNED THE IRISH ODYSSEY IS COMPLETE. YOU ARE WELCOME HERE AND SUGGEST YOU GET HERE WITHOUT DELAY. IF NECESSARY WILL ADVANCE NECESSARY FUNDS AND GIVE YOU OPPORTUNITY TO WORK OFF OBLIGATION.

In 1950 Mr. Wright and the Fellowship prepared an extensive exhibition called Sixty Years of Living Architecture. Complete with models, photo murals, original drawings, it travelled to Florence, Zurich, Paris, Darmstadt, Rotterdam, New York, Mexico City, and Los Angeles. Before its May, 1951 European opening at the Palazzo Strozzi, in Florence, it was shown in Philadelphia under the sponsorship of Arthur Kaufmann of Gimbels. Nearly one thousand original drawings were exhibited at this opening.

Unbeknown to Mr. Wright, these original architectural drawings and renderings were taken to a professional photographer in Philadelphia and photographed. The sponsors of the exhibition intended to give the photographs to Mr. Wright and to deposit the negatives in some "reputable East Coast university." When Mr. Wright heard about this he sent telegrams to the sponsors saying: "Stop at once this stealing of my work." Later, to G. M. Loeb, one of his clients, he wrote the following letter in which he explained where his work was ultimately to be housed.

January 29, 1951

My dear G. M.:

I intended to have a talk with you at the Philadelphia occasion but it didn't seem to materialize....

I would suppose you--(as everyone who really knows me)--knew what the struggle at Taliesin to establish my work for the next hundred years meant to us at Taliesin: our success or failure.

The F. Ll. W. Foundation has no other meaning than the sole repository of my life-work for whatever it may be worth for the next hundred years. I have no private fortune. My dependents I can only leave to our Foundation. If the Foundation cannot protect them by protecting itself for another half century (at least) the result will be tragic; not only tragedy to my loved ones, I believe, but also to the Cause of Architecture which I love as a whole with my whole heart....

As well as the two formal dinners with Mr. and Mrs. Wright on Saturday and Sunday evenings, we also shared Sunday morning breakfasts with them. After breakfast was finished, Mr. Wright would speak to the Fellowship on any topic that was under consideration at the time. He often spoke about the film shown the night before, or conversed with special guests, at the same time opening discussion to the Fellowship. All of his talks made clear the connection between architecture and life, for he himself saw no separation between the two.

At the time he wrote to G. M. Loeb, he also spoke to the Fellowship on this matter of his drawings and the repository of his life work. Out of this express wish has grown the archives of the Frank Lloyd Wright Memorial Foundation which now serve students and scholars from around the world.

January, 1951

"Whatever disposition made of my drawings, I intend them to be kept at Taliesin (West). That is going to be the Taliesin of the future--the repository of all those drawings and of that work. You may wonder why we are spending all this time and effort in expanding and making Taliesin more or less permanent. It is because it is going to be the only repository of this work in which you have contributed. If anyone wishes to learn about it or see it first hand authentically, this is where they are going to go to see it."

1952 (undated)

This is to certify that Mansinhji M. Rana was a Student of Architecture under my direction in The Frank Lloyd Wright Foundation for a period of three years and did excellent work. I am happy to recommend Mansinhji Rana without reservation and hope that he will be allowed to build in India, his native country, where I believe he will do very creditable work.

The Frank Lloyd Wright Foundation has been established as a cultural center and training ground for young architects from all over the world for the past twenty years. It is officially recognized by the United States Government as an Institution devoted to the education and teaching of the art of architecture and collateral crafts. The work of Frank Lloyd Wright and of The Frank Lloyd Wright Foundation is recognized throughout the world as the source of all architectural work now being executed and a letter of recommendation from this office is of more value than a degree of architecture from any college of Architecture in the world.

I respectfully ask that Mansinhji Rana be given the necessary license to practice architecture in India.

January 19, 1953
Senator Barry Goldwater
Washington, D. C.

Dear Barry:

Congratulations. Glad to have you out front for Arizona. Everybody will want to ask you for something. We ask a little consideration, ourselves.

There seems to be no little ignorance among U. S. A. officials as to just what our Foundation represents. There is no such confusion where foreign countries are concerned. They know our work when looking overseas toward us so we have continual applications from young architectural students from all over the world.

When looking outward our country is not so familiar with us at home for some reason--no doubt characteristic. But we are genuinely a cultural college doing an important work as you may see for yourself by reading the testimony in our local Wisconsin paper, copy herewith. Anyway, I think you know but you may need this collateral evidence for official purposes. Would you kindly expedite our appeal for certification by our own nation for recognition as and where we really belong--a College of Architecture. I have also written our Wisconsin Senator Wiley for same consideration from him. We are of Wisconsin seven months of the year and of Arizona for five months. We are now 21 years old.

We hope to be seeing you and Mrs. Goldwater sometime this winter, Barry. When you get home to try to rest will you let us know.

On March 20th, 1956, Mr. Wright once again prepared a statement of what the Taliesin educational experience meant to the cause of architecture and to the training of architects.

The Taliesin Fellowship

So far as his education goes, manifestly a creative artist is not to be made as a business-man or a scientist may be made. Frank Lloyd Wright, in love with Architecture and believing that architects were all that is the matter with architecture in our country, decided (about 1932 to be exact) to turn over all his work, property and prowess as an architect to a selected group of young aspirants who came to live and work with him and his family in a broad family relationship to share his work and so learn by doing. Domiciled in an atmosphere itself exemplar and appropriate to the purpose, the novitiates live a life of work and study under influences that constitute the nature of the genuine culture a modern architect would need. The philosophy of organic architecture thus becomes directly effective in the daily lives of a group of about forty novices.

Accordingly, a group of highly developed assistants has grown up around him of about eleven of what would be professor-status in any advanced architectural-college. Thus the now world-famous Taliesin Fellowship of The Frank Lloyd Wright Foundation came into existence. It has been difficult to hold the membership down. But sixty is as large as it has been allowed to grow. As it stands today, the Fellowship is something like a spontaneous U.N.; novices coming from all over the world for a sojourn at Taliesin North in Wisconsin, summer, and Taliesin West near Phoenix Arizona, winter.

There is a daily work-plan instead of a curriculum and continual cultivation in collateral arts and crafts. Experimental construction and actual building is continually shared by all. At Taliesin culture substitutes for instruction. Building especially and architectural design go on together. The actual planning of construction is always in progress and all share in it.

Some 136 young architects around the world are now there in architectural practice, having had the benefit of this practical association with Mr. Wright. The life and work of the Taliesin Fellowship is still young--about twenty four years old. Opportunity for experience in architecture and the arts has widened to work of greatly varied and significant character throughout the United States affording to the novices in the establishment of the Foundation since 1932, an unusually wide field of experience.

III

THE LUXURIES OF LIFE

To open a school in the Depression years invited serious financial problems. Tuition the first year brought in 23 times $650.00, and with this the Fellowship began to operate. Taliesin was outfitted to house more and more people and Hillside was expanded to include a new drafting room and further dormitory rooms. All of this expansion and remodeling required building materials, and even with the cost of labor somewhat reduced by the work of the apprentices themselves, stone masons and carpenters were also required.

If the apprentices fell behind in the payment of tuition the lack of money was felt all around, as the early letters in this section make clear. But in 1936, following the commissions for Edgar Kaufmann and Herbert Johnson, some of these pressures were temporarily relieved. It was always a temporary situation, however, and the life of the Fellowship depended heavily upon clients' fees as well as tuitions. The expenses of maintaining first one, then two, Taliesins mounted up, and student dropouts, all too often for money reasons, proved an added burden, especially during the years that no architectural commissions were coming in. At this time Mr. Wright travelled extensively across the country lecturing in order to bring in some money, leaving Mrs. Wright in charge of the Fellowship and the working out of its day-to-day life.

Grim as these pressures might seem, life in the Fellowship was good, even at the outset. Mr. Wright regarded beauty as the highest form of morality. He once said, "I can well do without the necessities, as long as I have the luxuries of life." By luxuries he means the things of beauty that gave meaning to life and evoked true culture. "Civilization" he many a time reminded us, "is but a way of life: culture is the way of making that life beautiful."

A bowl of wild flowers fresh from the meadows around Taliesin, an exquisite Japanese screen acquired when he was in Tokyo, an evening spent at dinner with family and friends, discussing all manner of topics relative to culture, philosophy and architecture, these were "luxuries" to Frank Lloyd Wright. His optimism in the face of difficult years and financial hard times was matched only by Mrs. Wright's. Together they shared their values and optimism with members of the Taliesin Fellowship. Gasoline might be scarce, motors and mechanical devices broken and needing repair, yet everyday life was plentiful with the experiences and learning of young, eager people. Food for the table was ample and fine, fresh from our gardens and farm. No matter how lean the times might be, the kitchen always flourished. And we were daily, under Mr. Wright's direction, perfecting those already beautiful buildings in which we lived. When his income had increased considerably, during the last ten years of his life, he invested in the reconstruction of and additions to the buildings in Wisconsin and Arizona. Both Taliesins were being assured a permanence they had never known before.

Therefore, despite the times when there was shortage of cash in hand, the Taliesin life was forever a beautiful one, accompanied by music and the arts and a deep appreciation of life in its fullest: hard work alongside good times, picnics, parties, outings into the hills of Wisconsin and the desert of Arizona. This continued joy in work and joy in life is as fundamental at Taliesin today as it was 50 years ago.

May 17, 1932
Miss Elizabeth Bauer
Vassar College

My dear Elizabeth:

Were it not for the fact that we need the tuition this year to get the buildings in shape--old and new--for opening this fall I should be inclined to say--come and take one of our honor fellowships. But if I start this now there will be no place to stop and no money to build with.

But I will say this: Send us your $300.-- at the earliest convenient moment and we will take care of you for the first year--perhaps partly here at Taliesin--partly at the Fellowship.

It seems to me $300.-- at the moment of starting is worth $670.-- once started?

I don't think Catherine need trouble to give you much but pin money once here, because your old clothes are probably too good and there is nothing to spend money for--except your personal laundry.

August 15, 1932
Abe Dombar
Cincinnati, Ohio

My dear Abe Dombar:

You are one boy I am glad to see come to the Fellowship--
As for answering your questions concerning the "preliminary month--"
A check for 135. should accompany your application to hold your place in the line--and the work begins formally October 20th, when half the balance of tuition fee is payable.

The balance for the first year is due Jan. 1st. I wish there was none to pay. For boys like you there should be a scholarship after the first year. I hope to able to manage this. But the first year unless we collect the tuition in full we can't carry on.

March 14, 1933
Ernst Benkert
Winnetka, Ill.

Dear Ernst:

I am writing you personally upon my own urge to do so concerning a money matter. I am doing it because the business of money and what relates thereto falls to my lot. The question I want to bring to you and to which I should like to have a decision from you is the amount left due on Steve's tuition; to be exact, $375.

I realize well the relation and motivation of this backing on your part of Steve's stay here and I think it is a fine thing for you to do. Now, Steve is my friend and I certainly regard you as one, which makes it all the more difficult to bring up the subject of money. But here it is and I hope you will understand our side as sympathetically as we understand yours.

The fact is that of all the boys here, Steve is the only one who has not paid up. The amount wouldn't matter so much but there is the time-element that enters at this period of our undertaking which makes it imperative to get the funds due. I doubt if you realize how severe the struggle is at times or I am sure you would have helped us out.

There is no "collection style" about this friendly letter, because, even if you can't raise the money we wouldn't ask Steve to leave. But that is beside the point. If the others had given us the delay that you, perhaps unwillingly, have given us, we would simply have had to send everybody home. That stands to reason.

So I am asking you if you will kindly let me know how and when you see it possible to manage the remainder of the tuition. The loud Hosannas that would rise to heaven upon the receipt of such concrete evidence of faith would warm your heart and make you feel amply repaid for the sacrifice it might have involved.

My best to Helen.

Fellowship tuition was originally $650., but this was raised the very next year to $1100. It stayed at that figure for the next twelve years, then again was raised to $1500. which stayed in effect until 1959.

April 22, 1933
Paul T. Frankl
Los Angeles, California

Dear Paul:

Peter leaves this afternoon to join his mother. He arrives in New York Tuesday evening at six thirty and the boat sails sometime Wednesday.

Maybe a good thing Peter goes along for awhile. He has flourished up to now here but if he comes back we will have to do a little planning for him. We can talk about that when the spirit moves.

You are still a trifle on the wrong side of his fees. The yearly fee is $1100.00--$650.00 down and $450.00 in four months. You wanted to pay this in monthly installments of $100.00 per month to which I agreed.

$200 was paid at one time but a month skipped thereafter--so $100 per month is what we have received up to now. The last payment received was February 14th which took Peter up to March 15th. You gave me $30.00 on March 15th payment leaving a balance of $70.00 due which would take $170 up to April 15th. There is $100.00 due to May 15th which would make $170.00 coming to us up to May 15th.

Peter arrived June 15th, 1934. So you have paid us $830.00. As I told you at the time, we only take boys for one year but if money is as tight for you as it is for us we'll forget the balance after you have paid $170.00 more to bring Peter up to May 15th.

I sincerely hope the breaks are your way from now on.

May 17, 1933
James Drought
Milwaukee, Wis.

My dear Jimmie:

I haven't written an answer to your plea because I haven't had money enough in my fist since, for one thing--and another--I have mostly been away or hard pressed on all sides.

We've never had a talk about money anyway--I assumed when you came here that you were coming to us as a regular apprentice on regular terms. But as time ran along and it appeared that father Drought was so hard up, I didn't say anything about it, and you never did.

So, like so many other things around about me, the matter just went by default.

However, if I had $60.00, Jimmie, you should have it--and whenever I get it loose long enough, you may expect it. Meantime consider it well enough applied on your education--together with the other sums it has cost to date.

There was no blue print fit to send to have you jot down your suggestions for planting. So that too went by.

I hope you are well occupied, somehow, and I hope it is not unlikely-- that Taliesin will know your loyalty and work again. We are getting on but--God--how we need money--the thing I should not have allowed to enter into the Fellowship plans at all--if I had known enough.

Maybe I can abolish it someday before it is too late.

June 26, 1933
Mr. Paul Beidler
Rome, Italy

My dear Paul Beidler:

We would like to take you into Fellowship but I have to refuse some thirty likely young men because they could not bring money with them.

We can't get the instruments we need into our hands in any other way. And our quota of Fellowships is full so far as we can go just now.

But I will say this. We will discount the future to some extent in this way.

If you will pay the amount of one year's tuition in advance so we can get some of the materials we pressingly need at the moment we will see you through the first and second year.

By that time the Fellowship will be in its stride and there will be many things we can do to enable you to go on the rest of the way if you should so elect.

There is no definite term or course here nor ever will be. I suspect a good many will find an agreeable and profitable lifework here in the Fellowship with us. But the matter is voluntary. You will be taking some chance in this as we would do.

You would have to decide to take it or not. If you want to come with us on these terms kindly sign the enclosed application, mail us a check for $200.-- and we will keep a place for you. The balance of $900.-- you could pay when you arrived or as soon after as would be convenient to you.

The final prospectus of the Fellowship enclosed herewith.

July 5, 1933
Mr. George Danz
Madison, Wis.

Dear George:

I wish I could take you on and certainly I would if I could. Our economic ways and means are too slim just now to try to house and feed any more young people. This is the plain fact.

Our condition may improve this fall and I might be able to give a different answer, but I can only say what I have said now. I want to thank you for your share in our music at Taliesin and hope you'll come again if you are near us this summer.

When money was in hand, Mr. Wright expanded his collections of Japanese and Chinese objects from art dealers in New York and San Francisco. These were part of the luxuries that meant so much to him, and that he generously shared with all of us. But when conditions demanded he would not hesitate to offer some of these works for sale in order that the life of the Fellowship might continue.

December 15, 1933
Miss Aline Barnsdall
Engaden, Switzerland

Aline Barnsdall was the client for whom Mr. Wright designed and built the "Hollyhock House" in Los Angeles, now the property of the

Cultural Affairs Department of the City of Los Angeles. Heiress to the Barnsdall oil fortune in Pennsylvania, she moved to Chicago where she was involved in pioneering work for the first Community Playhouse. When she left Chicago and came to Los Angeles she purchased a large tract of property called Olive Hill and planned a theater complex to be located around the Hill crown. The theater was never constructed.

Her daughter, Betty Barnsdall, was a member of the Fellowship from 1933 to 1936.

My dear Aline Barnsdall:

As you know, I would rather you had the silver screen than anyone else for many good reasons. It is yours on the terms you propose. $1000.--January 1st and $1000.00 March 1st. Shall I express it to you over there or shall I keep it in the vault for you until you return? Please wire concerning this. If you want it forwarded you should make some registration of it over there so if you pay duty it can be refunded when you take it back to the U.S.A. Maybe there is something I could do about the duty over here as it goes out?

Olgivanna and I will be very glad to have Betty with us as long as she cares to stay next summer. We both like her and the forty boys and girls here with us now are a fine group of young people with whom Betty will find much in common. The Fellowship is launched and if spirit counts it is going to be a great success. Of course we are poor. Money for the screen will enable us to keep the building going. We have been hung up for a while. I am sending along my copy of De Fries book with the Tahoe buildings and a translation, should you care to read it. You are right--. An "International" house would be as becoming to you as any packing box might be to an eagle. It is dying fast as a mode and taking its place where it belonged with standardized housing developments in big city slums. Romantic form in architecture is not inconsistent with good planning and sound construction. It is for the individual who wishes to really live and can live. The Tahoe buildings were good form arising out of the nature of materials, circumstances and site. I should say you had picked the place, up on a mountainside--that would be ideal for you. Why don't you buy the Emerald Bay property? There is nothing like it in the world for beauty I believe and it shouldn't cost much now? The Tahoe designs were tentlike and terraced--and belonged with the big trees around about them. I loved the whole thing and was broken hearted when I discovered the realtors were merely exploiting my name to serve their own ends. I am glad we will be seeing you in March--and hope you are well and happy enough. The boat on the Nile sounds like the sort of adventure to have. Am enclosing a few pieces about the Fellowship and send Olgivanna's regards. We are all well at the moment.

March 5, 1934
Alden B. Dow
Midland, Michigan

My dear Alden:

   My feelings in writing this letter to you are rather mixed. We didn't arrive at any very constructive understanding of one another nor of
anything together except in general effect, if that: Personal liking we had-
at least I did for you and Vada. And that is about all the basis there is for
what I am going to ask of you.
   Apprenticeship demands a higher type of ego and the power to
voluntarily bend the will--the harder the bending the better--to the
greater rather than to take the lesser. This higher ego of apprenticeship
we are learning to call aristocratic. By way of current education our current vulgarity has its main source in the petty ego--the ego that prefers
the donkey to Pegasus--unless Pegasus is its own. And by the signs of the
times it is not hard to see that Pegasus is donkey or there will be no
Pegasus.
   Never mind, the observation is prompted by what I have seen in the
working of our "educated" product against culture as we conceive it here
in the Fellowship. Whether culture is longer possible in the matter of Art-
Pegasus versus the donkey--I can't at this moment say--even for myself,
but I am encouraged, so far, nevertheless.
   Taliesin as a new American way of life has set up its standard against
the donkey ego that tore Architecture down as contrasted with the
Pegasus ego that hopes to set it up, believing that by way of voluntary
subjection to the ideal held in common--creative work may come back.
And believing in this is the only way.
   We have seen the deteriorating effects of every man's taking his little
shovelful of coal where he can and regardless setting up a little hell of his
own. Nothing greater than what has happened by way of it is likely to
happen. So here the struggle is between the current practice and the
higher service yet to be proved: the struggle between true abnegation
and the practice of self assertion before true abnegation has strengthened the spirit and developed the mind. Certainly as we have seen
economic and educational America our endeavor must seem hopeless.
   However that may be we must seek what help we can find from
those who will take the will for the deed. This implies on the part of
those who do help a greater generosity than faith. So let's say this appeal
is to your generosity.
   Here is the appeal--we have a chance to buy ready cut fine logs for
our summer work--709 of them which will yield about 70,000 feet of
lumber for our work next summer, practically all we need. They are only
a mile away and I can't get them without paying cash February 15th.

$350.00 for that item and we have only enough in sight to feed and fuel ourselves and gasoline our cars until next May.

I'll have to pay for saving the lumber. All told I'll have to pay about $750.00 for the seventy thousand feet laid ready to put into the building.

Now, there is one of the fine pieces of oriental sculpture (Yes, they are all Buddhas) here in the draughting room--a benign beautiful figure (gilded wood). I paid $1500.00 for it in Tokio in 1911. It is in fine condition. Would you take it over for $750.00? If so it is yours and maybe the Steins (I don't know how Jews feel about graven images) would like it against the wall of the library to the right as you enter the living room. Better still keep it for your own house. It is worthy and a small price--but I said an appeal to your "generosity" because I know that even at that you might not feel you could afford it or even like it as much as I do. Oriental sculpture of this type is perhaps an acquired taste. This emergency is here and in casting about in my mind for ways and means I have turned to you.

Can you do this for us?

Give my love to Vada--

To compound the problems with money, many apprentices elected to leave Taliesin shortly after their arrival because of family problems or financial difficulties. On occasion Mr. Wright himself would discharge a student.

Invariably, also, there were those for whom the rigorous and hard working life became too difficult to endure. The following list of rules, set up by Mr. Wright after the second year of the Fellowship, makes clear the Fellowship regimen.

January 4, 1934

1. We are here at Taliesin to work and to work hard. A day of hard work requires rather more than the normal eight hours of sleep. Adequate sleep is as essential to a healthy psyche as fresh air and good food. The curfew will ring therefore at ten minutes of ten o'clock. All members of the Fellowship are requested to promptly turn in when the lights are turned out at precisely ten o'clock. Those unable or unwilling to conform in spirit to the letter of this regulation will be invited to leave Taliesin.

2. The rising bell will ring fifteen minutes before breakfast at seven o'clock. With sufficient sleep everyone should be willing and able to appear promptly at the breakfast table every morning. On Sundays breakfast may be had any time up to ten o'clock.

3. Members of the Fellowship are requested not to seek the town for relaxation. If relaxation of this sort is necessary some quality that should

be present in work and fellowship is missing. The seeking of such relaxation in the circumstances set up at Taliesin will prove this. Either the life at Taliesin will be for the purpose of membership here, complete, or the member "town-relaxed" will be invited to return to the life of the town where, manifestly, he belongs.

4. But to avoid drawing hard lines for the present, exceptions may be made to the above regulations on appeal to Mrs. Wright or Mr. Wright for special occasions.

5. In the light of past experience it appears that the less the life of the private room and the town is practiced and the more the Fellowship foregathers on common ground the richer the quality of our social life will be for all concerned in this endeavor.

6. The outside work day begins at Taliesin promptly at eight o'clock, one hour being allowed each apprentice for breakfast and the upkeep of his room. The outside day at Taliesin ends at fifteen minutes to four o'clock when members will wash and appear at the studio for tea, thereafter working on studio projects until the support bell rings at six o'clock. Such work as may particularly interest the apprentice can be carried on there after supper. The more the studio life is a feature of Fellowship evenings the better.

FINALLY.   Man is essentially an appetite. Only as the satisfactions of appetite tend to uplift the individual and do not tend to sink him is there culture. Life at Taliesin is seeking earnestly for a natural basis for a natural culture. I hope all will be too much in earnest to put up long with thoughtlessness or willful disregard of the limitations fixed to ensure the growth of that life as a whole.

N.B. Emergency notices will appear from time to time which to some extent may modify these regulations.

TALIESIN: SPRING GREEN: WISCONSIN

November 8, 1933
Michael Meredith Hare
Hamden, Connecticut

My dear Hare:

I suppose the Taliesin Fellowship exists for independent eager spirits like yours. Your revolt does you immense credit and were I in your place I should consider that credit of more value than any other "credits" that Yale could furnish. I need not enlarge upon the contempt in which I hold what Yale in the name of the Beaux Arts does to the young man in Architecture.

I am glad to hear from Dek. He will be an architect of substantial quality someday but is victim just now of that defunct asset a degree from the Beaux Arts, imposed, I believe, by his father. But in coming here you would be an apprentice, not a student, and you would be put to work for what work would be worth to you.

But we are unable to take young men and put them shoulder to shoulder with us in this emergency without the apprenticeship fees we are all working with and living upon. They are--$200.00 with application for Fellowship, $450.00 when the apprentice arrives, and four months later, $450.00 more--$1100.00 in all for one full year's creative work. We take no apprentice for less than one year, but are willing not to reduce, but rearrange payments to suit special requirements as we can.

There is no "school year". Work is continuous experience. But a two weeks vacation may be taken when the work permits. There is greater freedom here than at college also more severe limitations in many ways. I should say the atmosphere here would be more wholesome and constructive in your life than anything I know about anywhere else.

Inasmuch as I am the architect whose apprentice you would be if you come, this may not sound quite modest. The truth seldom is I believe nor needs to be. I should be proud to have alongside a young man who will not give up what he believes to be right for any personal advantage whatever. That is the stuff of which the thirty young workers here now are made of.

If you see your way clear to join this group just wire us and we will make a place for you.

December 2, 1933
Michael Meredith Hare

My dear Hare:

I am glad you are settled and perhaps Columbia will work out as you wish. However, I see any text-book and class room education as a poor substitute for apprenticeship. And I see such a fool law as the one requiring a college degree for the practice of architecture as confining it to the inferior and inexperienced. I am sure such a law can't stand long and wouldn't worry about it because if a really good man went up against it, as many good men will go, there will be a way out. The whole license business has been a great hide-out for incompetents and quacks and is so regarded by the more intelligent members of the profession. Soon I believe that refuge will be removed and architects will have to stand upon what they have done and can do regardless of the scholasticism that has manufactured parasitic white collarites by the million.

December 29, 1933
Mrs. A. W. Burnham
Hubbard Woods

Dear Mrs. Burnham:

This is to wish you all a Happy New Year in the little loghouse in the woods and to talk over your son Willets.

Willets is something of a problem here. While we all like him I am not so sure this is the place for him at this period of his development. He is a maker of things, a restless promulgator of his own ideas. So far so good, but he is utterly lacking in any sense of responsibility and can follow through any task to completion only to show that he can do it. He has then had that and is looking for some other experience to devour.

Lately the desire for experimentation along the lines of personal sensation has waked in him--if it ever slept--and with a pint of whiskey got dead drunk and messed the place up rather nastily. Along the same lines, regardless of appearances he wanted to raise a beard to see how it felt and how long it would take it to grow. This made a further bedlam of his participation in the Fellowship. Then he was given the studio fires to attend to when there was no other fire to warm the studio and instead of taking it to heart and getting fire there before breakfast he was roaming about whistling contentedly some half hour afterward when I went in to work. No crime but an instance that is typical. He drove the truck and left it to stand over a zero night undrained which broke the block and cost me $60.-- but this is not complaint. It is an attempt at diagnosis for his own good--because certainly I feel responsible for the development of the young men who are here. For their own sake, mine no less, I can't encourage participation here unless it seems both helpful and appropriate all around. Now, I can't say what Willets' metier is in the short time he has been here. But I do not think he is to be an artist. I think he is mechanically minded and happiest when he can make something go--which might point to engineering or practical building and might be only a passing phase. For while Willets is 21 years old he is adolescent. Only now with the innocence of that period of youth--and its trying phases for those around him.

I do not want to say that Willets shall not come back if he wants to come or you want him to come. But if he comes he must expect a more rigid discipline of himself than he has shown and he must try to cooperate in a spirit more in keeping with liberty for all.

So far as I can see he can only be ruled by his affections for he has no respect for any living creature more than another and though conceited enough he has not enough real respect for Willets himself. This experimentation along the lines of personal sensation has two goals--one the insane asylum and the other jail. This makes me afraid for him and afraid of him. How do I know when or what he will do next--lacking any sense of responsibility or any respect for those with whom he is placed? But I am willing to set these fears aside if you think them groundless, for you know him better than I do--or could in a few months. So what this letter means is simply that Willets is up on the carpet for you to decide whether he shall come back here again--or shall not. If he comes we will do our best by him but he must get another slant on things and realize more co-operatively his own part in the scheme of things up here, such as it is. There is no one here who is going to follow him up or play nurse to some truant or recreant boy--whoever he may be.

There is room enough in liberty for every one but it requires some development to stand liberty or be safe in it.

Perhaps Willets hasn't development enough to be ready for it yet and will only feel the lack of discipline where discipline is coming from an ideal *within*.

May 3, 1934
A. M. Bush
Brooklyn, New York

My dear Mr. Bush:

At Alfred's earnest solicitation I am writing to intercede for him to save him from being another manufactured "white collarite." The essentials of earning a living are being developed in Alfred right here. They will be the same--city or country, present or future. To put him into competition with other thousands of his kind on the surface of things as they now run would be doing the boy a cruel injustice so it seems to me. He loves it here and is developing the manly qualities that insure his success in the kind of life that is coming. You might see this in yourself were you to see him in action, I believe. He is free, here, to develop from the ground up an individuality of his own whether he is concious of it or not--and meantime feel proud of a share in building up something of which he is a part and might be a part so long as he desired to be--his living assured.

Of course all that is impossible in any stereotyped college. Evidently Mrs. Bush's reaction was unfavorable to Alfred's place here. I didn't have opportunity to talk much with her but she seemed to appreciate the interest her son was taking in doing things that were actual but perhaps undervalued its significance to city life.

Might I suggest that since we have gone thus far with an interest in your son that you give us some explanation of your sudden resolve to take him out of here and throw him back into the stagnant city pool. That explanation would be helpful to us perhaps. You need not do this however unless you feel it. I suggest that were you to do so it might help us overcome the inimical point of view we are bound to meet everywhere in our effort to establish a better way of life here in America. And the rest of the argument I must leave to the young man himself. We are all fond of him. It is true he becomes impatient feeling his time limited and money especially so. But I can only say that what does soak into him here will do more to make him acceptable to future architects where getting a living is concerned than the more superficial "education" by way of which the "market" is already glutted. I know it is hard to see this far into the future especially so for Alfred being younger than most of the apprentices. But that should rebound to his advantage. It is to his credit that he "feels" enough of it to want to hang on.

Youth is pretty wise in instinct. I would rather trust it than adult wisdom--at the present time.

May 6, 1935

My dear Hank [Schubart]:

I have been in a quandary concerning your return to Taliesin. I want to be fair and frank with you. No one appreciates your good qualities more than I do but your kicking out last fall in the circumstances made me feel I couldn't really depend upon you. Your center of gravity shifted too easily. And already I felt that you would be smooth to me to my face and disrespectful behind my back to keep on good terms with your sense of humor....

I have the greatest respect and consideration for your mother and I do not wish to deny that you yourself have considerable ability and winning qualities if only you were trustworthy. You see, we can't live the life we live here so closely in common unless the Fellowships are more carefully chosen than they have been. I've learned a lot about that this past year, as things come to light. Of course you've knocked about the world a lot and contacted probably what I would consider pretty low types of men and women. Your view of life can't fail to be smirched by that. Now I don't care for angels with a lily even in one hand--but neither do I care for equivocal minded pseudo youth--young so far as responsibilities and abilities go and adult as far as attitude and sophistication goes. Your type of sophistication is not the type I want to live with nor desire to encourage in any way.

But you may have changed. Your mother says you have. I don't know why or how but I do know it might be so. Therefore I am unwilling to shut the door in your face even if the work here didn't need money which it does need more uncompromisingly than ever. So all considered I am going to say that if you care to come and try again complying with all the terms of the prospectus on a footing with the group of apprentices who pay full apprenticeship fees I am willing to try again hoping to see you otherwise than I have been seeing you.

However, I am not willing to make you any more financial concessions nor make any more allowance for your "adolescence". If you come in again you will come in as a man with full responsibility and because you want to share this work more than you want anything else, anywhere. No use otherwise as you wouldn't last three months.

Please give my best regards to your mother. I hope your Iraq interlude did something for you that you really needed.

1935 (undated)
Abe Dombar
Cincinnati, Ohio

Dear Abe:

Of course I am sorry you have to put your neck into the money-yoke because I don't think you should now--or ever for that matter. You are capable of a very much better fate and it seems very stupid to me that your mother should require it of you unless she and your father would starve otherwise which I doubt.

Taliesin's sons should belong to Taliesin for their own sake and the sake of a greater cause than merely family relationships which are everywhere pretty much the same.

If you could get some work worthy of your talents in which you might grow upon what you have absorbed here you might not be counted a total loss. But as it is I shall never take any more architectural sons in here who are first at the beck and call of mere family conditions.

I know this isn't Jewish. But I told this to a new boy from Michigan yesterday and will write into any applicant's acceptance hereafter a clause to that effect. I may invest Taliesin and myself in a likely boy like yourself and then have him ditch both Taliesin and myself when both need him most to help "ma" and "pa". I didn't foresee that. But I see it now and do not find it good.

I know the thing means a sacrifice for you and that you must get hold of some money to bring in bacon for breakfast for the city dwellers. But that doesn't change the essential waste of the whole business. I would remind you, son, of a talk we once had a year or more ago when you seemed backsliding a little and I asked you point blank if you intended to stay by me and go through with this thing and your reply was that you were going to stand by and "go through". At that time I was going to let you go if your answer had been otherwise and devote myself to some young fellow who would stay in line. I suppose you have forgotten that in the circumstances.

Nevertheless, affectionately yours,

With the building of Taliesin West in Arizona maintenance problems, and costs as well, doubled. Although more commissions were under way, money matters continued to be a daily problem. Gene Masselink was charged by Mr. Wright with the job of dispensing money. He also sent out the invoices to the clients and kept track of all financial transactions. All checks, however, bore Mr. Wright's signature. Right up to the time of his death he kept a firm rein on the finances of Taliesin.

One of Mr. Wright's clients once suggested that instead of having Gene, an artist and devoted apprentice, serve him as secretary and bookkeeper he employ a professional accountant. Mr. Wright replied that he would far prefer to have Gene work for him, even if it meant losing some money, than to have a..."professional who would, within a short time, soon own me lock, stock and barrel."

March 16, 1938
Eugene Masselink
Taliesin West, Arizona

Dear Gene:

I left the big envelope with papers in the car. Wish it had been put in my suitcase. But I had Mallery's address by Olgivanna and don't know if there was anything more of importance. If so, air mail it to the Lafayette.

I neglected to pay the wood man in Scottsdale and if the Andersons want to be paid--there is still $35.00 due from Cornelia and $50.00 from Jim.

Kevin owes some, too.

Keep peace in the family if you can and if you can't be the best fighter of them all.

1944 (undated)

Dear Gene:

Good news. But sorry it's a boy--

Getting your letters regularly and do what is necessary at this end.

How are you paying our bills? In what form, I mean, since I have no bank account. We will have to open one, of a kind, for the Foundation when I return which will be soon now. I wish you would get what you can together of the cost of running the farm before I turned it over to Wes. Say the last year or two. You probably have something--wages, taxes, etc. We never got much more than milk, eggs, butter, garden-stuff for the Fellowship--out of it. Sold calves and pigs--but no record probably. And probably no use making one except to show how well off we were when we had nothing--

I want to see where I was and where I am, that's all, and get back to independence of all fixed charges for upkeep so far as possible--working toward that from now on. To do it intelligently we must get as accurate a survey as we can, of what led up to the FOUNDATION. I don't know what you have on record. Let's have what you've got. Your memory is no better than mine. Good in spots?

Things are about as usual here. Weather wonderful. Olgivanna is brown as a berry. She seems to take to the Camp again--like the heroine she is--

My love to all the boys--and girls--All is not lost--yet--

Did you get a telegram from me asking you to send selection of ten mounted vertical Hiroshige. And a selection of ten from unmounted pile? If not send them parcel post at once.

1945 (undated)
Eugene Masselink
Taliesin, Wisconsin

Dear Gene:

We got on the train only because the passenger agent at the CNW&SP telephoned the train-dispatcher of NW Road and persuaded him to hold the train fifteen minutes for an eminent personality. Having a well known name is not always an inconvenience?

Thinking over the financial situation it seems too close as I hastily left it.

Never mind asking senior apprentices for gas money--I'll pay it.

And give Peter $50.00 more if he needs it. To do this have Glen and the Spring Green garage (and whatever other bills you can leave) sent to me at Phoenix.

The Fellowship obligations come first. I have money to carry on with when you all get to Camp [Taliesin West]. Because of seniority tell Ted Johnny has precedence if it should come down to a matter of "decisions".

I left the truck-trailer details to Wes who is to wire me the set-up he accomplishes--then I will forward check from San Francisco air mail-- including painting charges for both truck and trailer.

The repair bills on the Continental Zephyr at Kaysers can be forward- ed. Have a certain sum for household expenses, but watch Kay with ap- propriate admonishment. She is not very "tight" in spending money. Tell Svet to make herself comfortable. And the whole procession should get South as soon as possible. Nebraska is completely white--trees and all. This train is crowded--18 cars, a solid pullman train--but on time. Serve only two meals a day. Sailors and soldiers 75%.

I should look forward to a constructive and enjoyable four months at Camp. There is no reason why we should call in expensive help to close up Hillside, the House and the Studio. There must be an end to calling in dumb servants for things we ought to do ourselves. Thousands of dollars leak away that way....

Make no sidetrips for scenic effects at this time. We can indulge that on the way back.

I am most anxious to continue work on the Guggenheim and Johnson buildings.

Ted can make reproductions of Loeb drawings complete and send them to him as a present. Johnny can make another set of drawings of the San Francisco Funeral Homes with Ted's help.

You and Wes will have a lot to do to get to a proper "shove off". But I hope nothing will delay it unduly. If doubtful circumstances arise in gas- rationing, etc, consult Dave Bloodgood. I told Wes to go and see him on gen. prin.--.

That's all for the moment except Good Luck!

Mr. Wright was anxious to have a Steinway piano for the musical con- certs at Taliesin. The fathers of three apprentices, Mr. Tafel, Mr. Schubart, and Mr. Bush, were asked if they would contribute to making this acquisi- tion possible.

January 16, 1934
Henry A. Schubart
New York City

My dear Mr. Schubart:

I am going to ask you in behalf of your son's fellowship at Taliesin to be one of three New York patrons to take a one-third interest in a Stein- way concert grand piano we need badly and cannot get unless you do. It will mean only a payment of about $10.00 per month for twenty five months. We have had the matter up with Mr. Irion who wrote us at the suggestion of Mrs. Gaertner who at least took that much interest in us. The three patrons are yourself, Mr. Samuel Tafel, 31 W. 47th Street; and Mr. A.M. Bush, 2095 Union Street, Brooklyn.

I hope you will get together soon and see Mr. Irion as prompt action is needed if the piano is not sold before we get to him. Enclosed is a copy of the letter from Mr. Irion.

February 26, 1934

My dear Mr. Schubart:

The piano matter comes in sight again. Your last letter rather took the wind out of our sails--and we "hove to".

Now Mr. Russell of Wanamakers seems to have just the thing we want--whether the price is bed-rock or not you could find out.

At the moment we are in need of money and we have to fight the cold and keep going. Mr. Tafel has been trying to raise a little money for us and I have no doubt Mr. Bush would do the same thing. So if you can get together and send us this piano "toute suite" it will give our work an impetus we need.

Let me know what we would have to do in the matter and we will carry on to the limit of our ability--which we are hoping may soon increase.

Henry is a good boy and keeping fit. He will do good work someday. My best to you and Mrs. Schubart.

September 18, 1938
William A. Bernoudy
St. Louis, Missouri

Dear Billy:

We are glad to know you want to return to the life of the Fellowship--and are sure you would be a desirable addition.

If you feel as you do and think some help should be given you--so let's say that if you can contribute $500.00 per year for the next year or two we could probably put you on a senior basis where you would not be expected to pay anything but have a stipend to go on--enough to cover your personal expenses and eventually something more if we prosper as we expect.

N.B. Will not be coming to lecture in St. Louis this year--so far as I know..

February 4, 1940
Mr. Alfred Bush
Brooklyn, New York

Dear Alfie:

The Fellowship is now so organized that the bars have absolutely been put up and no one is entering the work except on the basis of the regular tuition of $1,100.00 for the twelve month year and the year is the minimum time. But inasmuch as you were here in the early days we would manage to take you on for a year--no less--for $600.00 which will help take care of your food and lodging at least.
    Please give my best to your father and mother--

March 8, 1940
Mrs. L. H. Ingraham
Rome, New York

My dear Mrs. Ingraham:

Thank you for your check. I am sorry that Gordon will not be able to stay his year out with the Fellowship. An apprentice just gets going about the end of the first year.
    Gordon has given a good account of himself--so far. How much talent for Architecture he possesses it is impossible to say at this time but I can say that if he so desired he might be a good one someday.

April 27, 1940
Alden Dow
Midland, Michigan

Dear Alden:

This choice clipping, sent me by somebody shows how wrong you were in your statement that one year with me is enough. This chap merely walked in one day and out again and got it all--?

My best to Vada and the little Dow-Dows.

Affectionately,

Will be seeing you all yet--I wouldn't wonder.

April 29, 1940
F. Bruce Maiden
Oakland, California

My dear Mr. Maiden:

Received one hundred dollars on account $450.00 due May first on Rowan's tuition.
Fellowship funds at this time are always lower than low. It is absolutely necessary that we get all the money coming to us which is little enough.
Can we count on the balance May first or if not kindly name a date so that we can arrange accordingly.

February 15, 1945
William Wallis Marks
West Geelong, Victoria, Australia

My dear Marks:

Get to Taliesin West--Scottsdale, Arizona (we are there now) as soon as you can and we will take you on.
I don't know when a letter from a young man (we have very many) has impressed me as favorably.
You will need very little money for Fellowship at Taliesin.

October 9, 1945
Joaquin Sicard
Flint, Michigan

My dear Sicard:

Your money is enough is the circumstances. Come along and get to
work.

1947 (undated)

Dear Gene:

Make a bill to the Canyon Park Inc. for $17000.00 and address and air
mail as on card enclosed--H.H. delighted. *[H.H. refers to Huntington Hart-
ford, for whom Mr. Wright designed a cottage group hotel and play
resort intended for Hollywood, but never built.]*

*From 1948 on, Uncle Vlado and Aunt Sophie were in permanent
residence at Taliesin West. Each summer a small group of apprentices
was assigned to stay on with them and help with the upkeep of the
buildings.*

May 14, 1948

Dear Vlado:

Received your letter regarding the boys. All right for them to work
with the sun but they ought to spend two hours at work after sun-down--
say from six to eight o'clock--instead of going to town. They are entitled
to the Ford only Wednesdays at their own expense for gas and oil.
Anything else is by your permission or invitation.
My best to Sophie and yourself--

N.B. I intended you to pay for everything connected with the upkeep
and occupation of the place after April 26th 1948--Butcher, Grocer,
Candlestick maker etc. etc. etc. (including fuel oil and bu-gas)...
I want to know thereby what it costs to keep up the place in summer.
Put bills where we have some record. Any outlay for building is not to be
included. We will send checks direct for that.

Cold and wet here since we came but better now. Olya *[Mrs. Wright]* wanted me to go right back--

July 25, 1949

Dear Vlado:

You don't hear much from us out there--but you and Sophie are very often in our thoughts. We wonder how you manage to dispose of all your leisure--knowing well how much there is to do. We have been pretty well this wet-hot summer (Gudmund suffers more from the heat here than he did there).

I am sure the continued high dry climate will set you both up for another fifty years.

I am enclosing a little change for the vest pocket (it must be empty). We expect to pay all your expenses.

Charles writes occasionally--there seems to be neither bottom top nor sides to this business of electric outfit for light and water. So much of our money goes for that transport that there is little left "on hand". Machinery is a hard game to beat. We will be coming out about November 1st and glad to be there with you.

The collection of pianos, both at Taliesin and Taliesin West steadily increased. A new cabaret theater was constructed at Taliesin West, and soon a music pavilion was constructed there as well. For these new pianos were needed. Already a fine Bechstein opera grand was purchased for the living room in Wisconsin. The fire at the Hillside playhouse in 1952 saw the destruction of the instrument there, and Mr. Wright placed an order for another Bechstein. Following the Kaufmann and Johnson commissions, Mr. Wright purchased a fine Pleyel harpsichord. By 1959 the list of pianos in both Taliesins would number a dozen, six of them fine instruments of the first quality.

February 14, 1950
Bill Deknatel
Chicago, Illinois

Dear Dek:

You are a good boy and inclined to help--but what we need is a grand old high class instrument a virtuoso could sit down to and not complain--one of the good old prewar instruments of the great line. A concert grand.

I guess Dorothy didn't understand.

We would pay up to a thousand for it but part of it would have to be a gift--deductible from income tax. We are a "Foundation" you know.

Part of the expansion of Taliesin and Taliesin West was the acquisition of more land whenever the possibility arose. Gradually Mr. Wright purchased all the farms in the valley that stretches out before Taliesin, thus returning the ancestral Lloyd Jones valley as founded by his grandfather to one ownership. He trimmed and cut trees, literally sculpted the landscape bordering the highway, put ugly power lines underground or hid them in the deep forests, removed open ditches, and created an exemplary model landscape.

In Arizona some of the original property was purchased outright, and some was leased from the State Land Office, all to protect Taliesin West from the inevitable encroachment. Here Mr. Wright preserved the desert with its natural features to illustrate how architecture and environment could blend together, thus providing an example on the Arizona mesa just as Taliesin served as an example to the Wisconsin countryside.

By the late forties and fifties, with commissions steadily increasing and work in the drafting room plentiful, all those years of desperate financial stress were surely left behind. In 1954, another "Taliesin" was added to the ones in Wisconsin and Arizona–at the Hotel Plaza in New York.

The Guggenheim Museum required so much personal supervision from Mr. Wright that it was decided to open a New York office. It took the form of an apartment at the Plaza, which Mr. Wright decorated in rich fabrics, oriental works of art, and black lacquer furniture that we made ourselves at Taliesin.

April, 1952
The Plaza
Fifth Avenue at 59th Street, New York

Dear Wes [Peters]:

Enclosed ch $9000.00 to Mrs. Hoyer–*[for land purchase for Taliesin West.]* (I think I paid her only $1000.00 down--but check contract--)

Be a little slow delivering the ck so I can cover with Anthony's check mailed to me today which I will immediately forward to the Valley Bank--

Get release properly--

I can't understand what went on in the bank acct. because I asked for balance ($9000.00) when I left and drew no checks on that bank since the plane fares to N.Y.--

Mrs. Boomer will perhaps play along--send me the Adelman plans air mail and revised figures on the house on the hill. There is a good deal there yet.

IV

CHOOSE YOUR ANCESTORS WITH CARE

Since the concept of a Taliesin-trained architect was directly opposed to the academic system of professor-student, Mr. Wright referred to us as "apprentices." But when he addressed us individually or in a group, or spoke more intimately about us, we were always his "boys and girls." It was a term which carried much affection, and indeed the greater part of his letters to the apprentices are signed "Affection."

He spoke of Mrs. Wright as "Mother." The inference of a type of parental association is a strong one. Taliesin was—and is—a closely knit family in many ways, as these letters reveal. When asked on various occasions what the secret to success would be for someone, he frequently answered, "You must choose your ancestors with the greatest of care."

Mr. and Mrs. Wright became our chosen ancestors in this deeper sense of spiritual mother and father. The letters that follow in this section depict Mr. Wright's concern for the well-being and the development of his apprentices, not only during their stay at Taliesin but also concern for their future. He warned of the pitfalls resulting from too much eager ambition in the race to rush out and get "a job". He told us many times of the lure of that first job: an apprentice would get a commission, design a home or commercial building, get himself published for the first time, and then sink into obscurity ever after.

As time went on, former apprentices frequently sent gifts on the occasion of his birthday, June 8, and Christmas. He once wrote to his daughter Iovanna, "Your scarf was fine for me—very desirable and in good taste. I guess you know what I like. It is hard to give me a present, I *know." But he was genuinely appreciative of the efforts to please him on these traditional occasions.*

January 9, 1933
Mr. Samuel Ratensky
Brooklyn, N.Y.

My dear Sam:

We are all sorry to hear of your accident and we hope your holidays, at least we're not spoiled. A horse is not for you--my boy, try something else. You have entered on a chapter of experiences since you came back home to us from New York last year that is taking you off your toes where you were up and coming when you first came and is letting you down bump after bump?

I think the state of feeling into which you have gone for one reason or another will invite the untoward and leave you defenseless against it if you drift. I do not think it is for your own good to droop. A weakness in your character, maybe, is showing, that needs bracing, I've been thinking over you somewhat, Sam, since you left Taliesin--because of affection for you.

When you left for home if you were as you were when "up and coming" when you first came you would not have missed the Davidson's markets and farm-units which were due and went off in good shape--(12 sheets) January 1st. That would have been more fun than anything else and duty otherwise dubious.

I have you now at arms length--and enough in perspective to see that I made a mistake for us both when I did not let you go when you wanted to go and had pretty generally informed the place you were going before I heard a word from you about it myself. No man, unless very strong, entirely recovers from a lapse of morale like that, whatever the cause, and I do not believe Sam is that kind of strong. He is strong in his desires, emotions and affections but morally weak. I could go on to mention many causes of your loss of spirit here and the lack of the necessary morale to go forward in the confusion of the present struggle to the reasonable triumph ahead. Some I could advance might hit the mark, the nearest being that you were a privileged young man at the outset and felt set aside when the others came in a huddle. It take guts and vision and a deeper loyalty to the cause here than I believe you now possess to carry through the rough emergency into the calmer waters ahead with profit to yourself and the work, nor do I believe, though I do believe in your pluck, you are a mariner of that type.

I am too sentimental myself about my boys here when they are with me to get the perspective I often do get when they are off at arms length as you are now, and this perspective shows me, Sam, that you would better follow your instincts if you can manage it and go over to Europe next spring for some more intimate knowledge of the thing they are doing over there.

You have had a good deal from Taliesin already--in first hand contact with the thought that built it and still moves it to build. You were a loyal son for some considerable time, but time now for you to take fresh hold of yourself and go on your way--as your desires draw you strongest. This is not saying I do not want you to come back to us. But saying you should come only when the spirit moves with a clean sweep and you feel that your place is here with me in the work that is ours. Whenever that time comes now or in a year or two you will be welcome. For the next several years Taliesin needs every man up on tip toe and coming along-head up and singing--. A large order, Sam? Yes, but one no harder to fill than many filled before. So, here's to you, son. Get well and get out where the birds are singing in your heart. You should have caught enough of the singing here to lead you on and cheer you on in your next steps in your great adventure.

Every man's life is a great adventure to him.

Affectionately,

October 21, 1933
Mr. William Beye Fyfe
Chicago, Ill.

Dear Will:

Replying to your note--
1. The work out of which a man makes his living should come first.
2. A true apprenticeship means allegiance.
3. A fellowship of apprentices requires a common sacrifice to the common objective.

In the articles of apprenticeship as specified "a vacation of six weeks if and when the work permits."

If all were to do as you have done, and many have already done so with no rebuke from me, I can't see much order or dependability in any working body we might attempt to become. We would be free for all and the devil for the hindmost. It is not so good to get dressed up and go looking for your chief to "tell him" you are off for a couple of weeks to paint somebody's--anybody's--house.

When you come back we will talk it over and try to get the thing on straight. I am sure you meant no dereliction and thought none. But something is lacking somewhere.

September 28, 1934
Aline Barnsdall
Palos Verdes, California

Dear Aline:

Am sending you the book--it is my own presented by the author so please return it. Why don't you buy Emerald Bay for a song and give this fresh start to California Architecture. It would go well with a better social order. Somehow I can't much believe in Sinclair's sincerity apart from the man's desire to shine. He has certain ideals that discipline him and so may hold him to the work he has cut out for himself. But I've never yet known a radical who did not change when the established order took him up and put power in his hands.

Money acts the same way upon them. I could cite cases within my intimate experience and know of none otherwise unless I can prove up myself. If "government" put its eggs in my basket I don't believe I would compromise, but looking around at the effects about me I should worry too! Of course the visit to the President had its effect upon your man. The American revolution is on and will be more a change of thought than bloodshed. But money--I suspect--isn't going to be worth as much if much at all.

So--better get the things you need or desire as things while money will buy them. I have a stingy cousin, head of the school of commerce here who got a new Steinway the other day--feeling that way himself. It is the first time we ever agreed about anything in our lives. He slaves and saves. Look at me!

The only way to "manipulate" money is use it to make two blades of grass *grow* where one or none grew before and preferably where ideas are concerned. So here's more power to you to get rid of yours in time.

The "Kid" *[Betty, her daughter]* is doing pretty well just now. I was terribly hard on her. But she is as completely "gone" on "Bud" as ever you were on her father. That puts another face on matters for me and I'll do what I can to see them through. Bud is a good fellow if drink doesn't get him. But hard liquor is a frightful cheat and changes everything with more subtlety than it ever gets credit for. There isn't much chance with it because deterioration is "interior" and for so long invisible. It is largely in the stamina. Some call it moral fibre. The human race never gets anywhere because nature put too high a premium on pleasure below the belt and not enough upon the mind which doesn't seem to mean much to her anyway. Vanity is only this pleasure we take in ourselves.

I'll try Maginel out on the house but how can you endure urban stupidities for more than three weeks. The only region more healthful and beautiful than the Tahoe region is the all year round climate of the far Northwest--the most beautiful part of our country and destined because of its beauty and wholeness to be the future center of culture for our country. I mean Oregon and Washington with their beautiful seas, snow capped mountains, forests, fruits and flowers. If the good "God" had cast my role there how lucky I should now consider myself. As for traveler's interest in our great midwest there is none except in spots and in the way of going. It bores me too. And what bores me most is the god damned dollar minded view of the universe which begins when slaving parents teach their children to *save*.

The success ideal here is false as hell. You are seeing its fruits right now. Physically however our country is more beautiful than any other. And cheese and common wine is pretty good fare I should say but then so is chicken roast, good coffee and a piece of apple pie?

If F.LL.W. had been born in Holland he would have been a Dutchman. Can you imagine it? Or an Italian? Sooner a Chinese, I say.

"Homesick" in your life means I imagine a desire to get going. Why don't you get an amphibian plane filled up with modern comforts--with art-gallery or propaganda trailer and do the world in ninety days? If you were conscious that you could fly that way you might learn to value the repose that comes to rooted things.

Maybe you are orchardistic or something.

I am interested in your helpless thousands only as the light can break for them from their own "*above*". Outside that I think the sooner the remorseless appetite their god originally made them is extinguished the better. A good animal interests me, and so far as a human being is a good one and lets it go at that honestly, I am mildly interested. But we compare badly with the other animals on any such basis. We've got to be more, and are uneasy about it because by no means sure, and our fake philosophy has fallen apart where mind is concerned.

So long as you have to "take one servant" anywhere you've given the hostage to fate that enables life to make you miserable.

"Servants" are essential vulgarity and spoil life. Let's modify life to send them on their way to selfhood so we ourselves can have a change in that direction. Parasites be damned of either variety.

May 14, 1934
Mr. Frederick Langhorst
Elgin, Illinois

My dear Fred:

I went to look for you and found you gone. I didn't realize that you were already on your way when so casually you told me you were off. Of course I realize what a blow the loss of Rogue means to you. It was because I realized what a dog might mean in your life that I made an exception and allowed you to have one here. So perhaps I am to blame for your affliction. Some day you will lose your Father and your Mother and nearest and dearest of kin as I have and probably this trial was given to you to gain fortitude to meet such losses. I didn't want to sympathize over much with you because I have found sympathy debilitating and of little help. Courage and action are best. Work is all, when trouble comes, so I have found it, but natures differ and this may lead you to consider deeply your own ways and means to future life. I hope so and my dear boy whatever you see clearly ahead of you as best for you, to that "best" Taliesin subscribes. I have wanted to see you get hold of yourself and triumph over certain weaknesses apparent to me in you--like your inability to command yourself in the morning--like starting a new thing every so often and never really carrying one of them through. And I think you lacked co-operation from your fellows in your endeavors here because of a certain impatience and lack of sympathy with those under or near you. Nevertheless I subscribed to you and liked you and counted on you--and had faith you would grow out of over-education into a quiet faith in yourself and a love of work into which you could put yourself. It is true it was all in your care a little late. But of all the lads here you seemed to catch the ideas most clearly. You have done good work here. It is appreciated. It counts. Yet something was lacking. Was it the ability to follow through? The guts to stay put--hell or no? Sometimes you went through and I rejoiced. Things were looking up. At any rate Rogue will have been one more trial added to the other put upon you here by your own character--call it fate--and by our own struggle to achieve a victory over circumstances. We will achieve the victory we anticipate but never wholly. Only a part of what we dream becomes objective. The best part, maybe, always is subjective. I noticed of course your drifting for a month or so past--but saw no other way than to be kind and let you work it out yourself. It is the only way, Fred. Taliesin has been your sympathetic home for a couple of years--son--and when you feel like coming back will be again. And in any case remembers you and wishes you well in whatever you do.

June 17, 1946
Royden Dangerfield
The University of Oklahoma, Norman

Dear Mr. Dangerfield:

I think that Fred Langhorst would be able to admirably fill the position that you mention.
I hope you employ him.

August 20, 1934
Mr. Paul Frankl
New York City

Dear Paul:

I rather expected you would call up from Chicago and was a little worried when we didn't hear from you. Conscience troubled me a little keeping the lad when you wanted him but when I looked around there was no car available anyway. Ours weren't ship-shape, Marybud and John were in Marquette, etc. etc.

Pietro *[Peter, his son]* is doing very well. He has dropped some of the defense complex he had when he came (his ultra self-assertion) and is really a good boy. He is liked by everybody. He stopped me the other day as I was rushing away to say: "Mr. Wright, if we go to Arizona next winter who's going to put up the ice?"

A long shot for a kid--that.

He's had a birthday--18th. His mother sent him $30.--. He has bought a hunting knife and wears it weekdays and Sundays on his hip. Wants to buy a horse etc. etc., I've headed the boys into abstractions and Peter brought in one and laid it on the table. I've enclosed it.

He'll come out all right if he isn't pushed. A boy like Pietro should be allowed to "come along".

Yes, Ray Hood was a good egg. Architecture needs about ten first class funerals of the higher-ups more than it needed his.

The Monograph referred to in the following letter is the publication TALIESIN, *a magazine containing essays on architecture, on the education of an architect, as well as illustrations of life at Taliesin and some of the architectural models that were being made in the early years of the Fellowship. Many articles were written by members of the Fellowship as well as by contributors outside of Taliesin. One special–and now very rare–issue of the magazine was devoted to Broadacre City, called "The New Frontier," copiously illustrated with photographs of drawings and models.*

September 20, 1934
Philip Holliday
Fairmont, Indiana

Dear Phil:

I know it came hard and close so many thanks for the subcription to the Monograph. We are at work upon it and the first issue isn't far away.

Any time you can use a "certificate" I'll send some good and I trust-- helpful words concerning your stay here. Let me know when and just for what so I can make it appropriate. I think Taliesin must have done something for you in point of general culture although I never felt in talking with you that you had clearly grasped just what it was all about anyway.

And I feel that you, in common with several other Experimental College boys I've known, had your critical faculty developed far beyond your judgement. The attitude of criticism rather than appreciation seemed to rule you and cheat you.

However that may be, we all miss you and wish you were back in the family at work. More and more I see the Fellowship as a family--to continue at work in the work of all branches of architecture and allied crafts as a producer of art works and promoter of a new way of American life.

But I've yet found not much fellowship material, that is to say fellows more interested in their place in the work here than in what is going to happen to them in the way of a job when they get out. With their eye on that "job" there's not much growth in them here nor for us in them. Let me know how you get on--or don't get on either--and you may count upon any help I can give you. We have several desirable new apprentices, among them a student of painting for some years abroad and son of Pittsburgh's "Marshall Field". He seems excellent material as does a young woman from the same city. [Edgar J. Kaufmann Jr., and Cornelia Brierly]

November 12, 1934

My dear Edgar [Tafel]:

Word came from your mother that you left New York last Wednesday for Taliesin but Gene has just told me that you were at Midland with the Dows.

Now the Fellowship faces action on a scale and with an intensity that will allow no dillydallying on the part of anyone belonging by spirit and purpose to this group. Tom Maloney writes we are to make a model of

Broadacre City for the big New York show and offers $1000.00 for expense money. Stanley Marcus has commissioned us to build a home for him in Texas. We have a memorial chapel to build near Madison and we have all the work of getting the caravan (pioneers) in shape for Arizona beside our own upkeep and growth here.

I know you've been sick and are probably not yet fit to work. It takes three times as long to recover from a holiday I've found as the holiday itself takes.

I am none too pleased with your extended neglect of your fortunes here already. If Alden will give you a job--I should hate to lose you but would say amen to the not unexpected. He offered a job to Bob Mosher. And if Alden needs help and you want to give it to him--make up your mind and we'll get you out of our mind.

But it is time for you to fish or cut bait....

You can work if you want to work and if you come back you will have to do your most. Fair warning too that "adopted sons" are required to show respect to their parents especially behind their backs.

No one understands your good qualities more than I do or likes you personally more, probably. But that isn't going to "frank you" where the life and endeavor of the Fellowship goes with you. It can go on without you but it can't go on with you in it and not loyally of it. Either you are of it and for it or out of it. And this applies to everyone else here now as it never did before.

If I can count on your loyalty in this sense--come back. If there is any half hearted feeling about it you would do better to stay where you are because it would only be a question of time before you would have to go somewhere anyway.

I am writing you this to save you any false moves that might embarrass us both.

I shall expect to hear from you forthwith.

Give my best to the Dows.

November 30, 1942

TO WHOM IT MAY CONCERN:

This is to certify that Edgar Tafel has been a member of the Taliesin Fellowship working for me for about ten years. He is capable and intelligent. I recommend his services to anyone interested in building good buildings.

December 4, 1934
Aline Barnsdall
Palos Verdes, California

Dear Aline:

Your little daughter is in a state of mind--needs your blessing I guess. So I thought you might come here now and save her the expense and "time out" of a trip out there to see you.

Also I selfishly wanted to see you myself. Another thing I feel I did Bud an injustice in the circumstances as they stand now when I last wrote you. After all--or before all--he is a good fellow--has definite possibilities if he can be kept at work here for a couple of years. He is pretty green and a little putty-ful right now. I think the young people should have only enough money to keep them comfortable here or in some similar place where they can grow up in a great work for two years more at least. They need to settle down on that.

To discuss these questions beside your daughter's state of mind which I take it is a state of heart--meaning she loves you and is deeply worried--was why I wanted you to come here. I have sciatica myself occasionally and have found relief at such times by lying naked in the sun, eating yogurt (Bulgarian sour milk) drinking lemon water freely and not worrying--much.

Cold or heat hasn't much to do with it, I believe. The state of mind has a good deal of effect, also acidity of the stomach.

Since receiving your telegram the young daughter is herself determined to start for Palos Verdes at once.

I couldn't restrain the youngsters from getting married and I can't stop them now it seems. So I guess they are up to you. You and your daughter are both pretty willful.

I hope we will see you when you are better.

May 2, 1935
Phil Holliday
Sugar Grove, Illinois

My dear Phil:

Thank you for both your letters. The second brought the "six months" (it was several anyhow) to an end.

You of all the boys here had least of myself and because of your own reticence where others were more forward and in consequence you probably got less of the idea of organic quality in thought and action that I feel the place we call Taliesin should stand for. Of course we don't reach the ideal. But striving for it is enough to give the same health and vigor spiritually that we enjoy as a reward for striving physically.

I am not sure but that you were, and still are, looking for miracles. No very happy lad at heart--rather cynical and pessimistic by nature but an idealist too if I'm not mistaken you don't get the right approach to the miracle, if you must have one. The country is one of course in the right sense. Couple with it a warm personal belief in an ideal and a work for it that one can grow up with and other "miracles" will mark every hour of every day if one doesn't get one's self too large in the foreground and shut out any breadth of view.

It is something to be "clever". Most lads are satisfied to make that seem important. Being clever one can be as much more than clever as one *is* within himself a healthy developing human being. This humanness is what is lacking in most wisecracking, sarcastic, hypercritical youths "educated" under present leadership. In other words so many young are pseudo-adult. The sweet, swift-spirit of youth they have lost or never had.

Now you see by this so far that feeling is the beginning but not the end of painting and architecture.

Good painting is good architecture, with all the tenets held here at Taliesin in place. Those tenets you did not get into proper place where painting is concerned while here but the fact that you were upset and still trying to get right side up is a pretty good indication that you eventually will.

Abstraction as I've tried to inculcate it here is nothing to be quickly grasped even as an ideal. To work it out requires patience and time.

Experience is more an inner than an outward affair. This is because reality is within. In this realm of the within the abstraction that heightens reality to the eye is to be found. The degree to which you may keep abstract in what you do depends upon your own development. I don't think it should have anything much to do with the state of development of those around you. They are the "gallery" only to use that figure of speech. You are your true audience.

The less direction you take from the outside the better for you. The more you hold consciously to right ideals and try to verify your sense of them by working away in accord with them the better.

Now it's true that living and pursuits should be one and would be were we not struggling to emerge from the injustice of robbery and slavery. I wanted Taliesin to emerge into some such life for the Fellowship as that and the only way I could see to get there was to do a little robbing and enslaving myself but with that end in view.

In other words I had to have a little money and if I got it had to get it by grafting all I could (believe me no one can graft on it very much for an ideal) on "the system".

The boys brought what they could bring. Quite a number of them have been unable to bring any as you know. I've never made a point of money except as a "desperation".

Your natural place, were you to feel it so, is here. And if you were to feel it so to be so I am sure I should like to have you here, money or no money. I feel your place is here because of what you might impart to us of fellowship and sevice to our ideal and because of your own likable self. All this.

But perhaps more important, because I feel no painter could grow up outside of architecture in the sense that we practice architecture here and be a great painter.

November 6, 1935
William B. Fyfe
Berlin, Connecticut

Dear Will:

TALIESIN will issue in about ten days and your copy will go where you have designated. I wish you were at work upon the next issue.

Taliesin misses you. Perhaps life may shape itself so that your apprenticeship may be resumed and grow into mastership. I find myself with a feeling of something gone wrong whenever my boys go out before I am ready to have them go. This was probably the best place for you, all told, for another five years.

But man proposes and the money mind disposes--or what have you on your mind? Let me know how the game goes from time to time. Something may turn up.

I saw your Mother at the Patio dinner the other evening which you also should have attended. I asked Grace to try gold leaf on the window openings and a gold swastika to honor the work. She promised. The cabinets you worked out looked unexpectedly well. And outside a little extremity of angularity the effect of the whole place is a credit to us all. We all wish you good luck.

January 3, 1935
John E. Lautner
Marquette, Michigan

John Lautner came to Taliesin in 1933 and remained in the Fellowship for six years. Mr. Wright sent him on a series of supervising jobs, first in Michigan and then in California, where he now practices.

My dear John:

Pretty tough, eh Son?

I don't know how far down you've gone but believe it is all in the damned little gall bladder you inherited and don't overlook the fact that a self-indulgent disposition always goes along with it. Don't let them baby you up there John.

You simply have a little "stop light" to heed and I hope you heed it. Holidays are hell. Look out for them. They are so much worse than work. Ask the gall bladder.

I, for one, shall miss you very much on the trip west and also before because I have been looking forward to work on the plans of the house A.B.R. *[Abby Beecher Roberts]* with you.

But I suppose that can wait for your recovery. Too bad you had to cave in at the point where you range up alongside your chief for a real "set-up" in the drafting room. But here's hoping you throw this all off and get into your manly stride.

The women will have you on your back whereas you ought to have them on theirs.

My love to your Mary--Mary quite contrary--

January 10, 1936
Abe Dombar
Cincinnati, Ohio

My dear Abe:

I am sorry not to have answered your letter sooner. It deserved a prompt answer but I think you know how it is. There was no time to negotiate a lecture but we will do that next April or May on terms you propose.

I suppose Benny keeps you posted on the affairs of the Fellowship and you know therefore more than I do about them. *[Benny refers to Benjamin Dombar, his brother. Both Benny and Abe were Charter Members of the Taliesin Fellowship.]*

This note is only to let you know my good hopes for you. The Fellowship has missed you and it would be a great pity if nothing commensurate compensated you for leaving. We are going into the small house business as a Fellowship next Spring in earnest, meaning to build them for our neighboring cities in large numbers. We leave for Arizona tomorrow morning at four A.M. and I shall miss your cheerful self.

My best to your parents.

July 18, 1939
Michael Kostanecki
Warsaw, Poland

Dear Michael:

Glad to hear from you again. Was afraid something might have happened as there was no word of you nor from you since you last left Taliesin except vague rumors of an accident to your mother and brother.

I've read your historical essay on "the Chicago group". I suppose it does look that way if you look at it quick from the outside. But like all history I guess the "inwardness" of it doesn't come out very clearly in any survey. It is as good a survey as any however, and perhaps good enough.

History is never anything but the outside view--"ipso facto" you know. Hence, unless powerful interpretation (rare indeed), History is bound to be misleading, so I believe.

You left out Buffington of Minneapolis (the inventor of the steel frame for building), Van Brent and Howe of Kansas City (the station builders), Major Jenney, S.S. Bemen etc., etc., from the "Chicago" group. St. Louis, Detroit, Cleveland, San Francisco--all had good men in line with native effort at that moment. The list would be long as I was familiar with it where I was working.

Le Corbusier is ambiguous in your category to say the least. And what I am and where is but darkly inferred--the ghost.

Distrust History more and more--Michael--even your own!

I am sorry we don't see more of you. Are you coming over to the New York fiasco perhaps? There were many commendable things in your study of conditions however--I don't want to deprecate what is apparently a conscientious effort.

Thanks for sending it. And my best to you, my boy!

[Michael Kostanecki was last seen in Poland during the Nazi occupation, but has never been heard of since.]

June 13, 1938
Philip Holliday
Oak Park, Illinois

Dear Phil:

Thanks for the linens on the birthday. They are much appreciated. Why not come up some time this summer for a visit?

January 30, 1939
Noverre Musson
Findlay, Ohio

Dear Noverre:

Thanks for your letter. You were not wasted on Taliesin nor was Taliesin wasted on you I am sure.

January 30, 1939

TO WHOM IT MAY CONCERN:

Noverre Musson was a member of the Taliesin Fellowship--under my direction, for about two years from September 1st, 1935 to June 30th, 1937.
I consider him faithful, conscientious, and intelligent. I believe him able to carry through satisfactorily to all concerned anything he might undertake.

January 18, 1941
Mr. F. Bruce Maiden
Oakland, California

My dear Mr. Maiden:

I quite understand your feeling about Rowan's marriage being the father of four sons myself. But the marriage seemed to us all so appropriate for Rowan, knowing little or nothing of his financial circumstances except that he was favorably "fixed", we all contributed our best wishes and good-speed to the romance.

I still think Jerry is the right prescription for your son at this time. And if you are "hard up" now--and can keep Rowan on--we will do our best to keep Jerry at his side in the Fellowship.

"Romeo and Juliet" mentioned in the next letter is the slender, tall windmill tower that Mr. Wright built for his two aunts, Nell and Jane Lloyd Jones, on the hilltop above the Hillside Home School. Constructed in 1896, Mr. Wright termed it "my first example of engineering-architecture."

February 16, 1941

My dear Jim:

I've owed you a note for a long time not knowing just how to say what I wanted to say.

Often I have wondered what you thought you were doing when you withdrew your active support from your Fellowship after the academic period of four years, took what opportunity you had and with your little shovelful of coals started a little hell of your own in the bosom of your family. Your mother was ill and needed you, I thought, and let it rest there.

Then you showed me what became of your devoted defection--an utter sellout to convention which I again ascribed to family. Although I could not refrain from the recollection that I built Romeo and Juliet for my family under similar circumstances.

Now you are building outside the family, annexing Victor, a disgruntled apprentice to help you. And you write me to say that you are carrying on my principles like the loyal son I imagined you to be.

When a boy has a little money and opportunity it seems he can't wait to get his own name on it and be free of the dubiety of apprenticeship--preferring dubiety of performance. Well, I have not seen that the cause of architecture is greatly forward by this ornery manipulation--or ever will be. I see it only as inevitable in the circumstances in which our young men come to be what they are--which is not at all what they think they are.

No, I think many of the more humble faithful spirits without means of their own at the moment will eventually be the stronger ones contributing most to integral architecture in the long run. Advantages most often turn out to be disadvantages in our equivocal "system", I am sorry to see--or is that simply nature maintaining her equilibrium?

As I think you must know, you have my true affection and a deeper regard than perhaps got to you while you were with me in the

Fellowship. I am sorry it could not have built up into cooperation, in a beautiful way of work and life for you and for the Fellowship. Why this could not be you probably know. I do not, except as I put it to you now.

January 13, 1942
Cornelia Berndtson
Pittsburgh, Pennsylvania

While at Taliesin, Cornelia Brierly married Peter Berndtson, who had also joined the Fellowship. They later set up a partnership practice in Pittsburgh, but Cornelia returned to Taliesin in 1957 and has remained ever since. Their two daughters, Anna and Indira, also live at Taliesin and are members of the staff.

Dear Cornelia:

My Christmas present was just what I needed and goes along with the others to make a notable collection from you.

Of course we all miss you and Peter and baby Anna, a lot. But I suppose independent speculation beats Fellowship Co-operation, at least for a while?

I don't believe anything can compare with our life here now. We've rebuilt the camp and it is not only dry but exceedingly beautiful as a background for group life with fine feeling throughout I believe.

I hope the Spokane investments pan out but whether the present is a good or a bad time to make them I don't know.

At any rate your work and fellowship for many years is built into what we are doing and no doubt you will someday be very proud of the fact.

June 12, 1942

Dear Cornelia:

We were really glad to hear from you and receive a tangible proof of your consideration and ability too. I have said that you of all the girls coming to Taliesin got most out of it in spirit and in deed. I like the rug very much. And I had always intended to make you captain of a follow-up brigade to furnish the Usonian houses and housebreak the owners to occupy them gracefully and comfortably. But the babies came along too soon for our economy.

Heigh-ho!...My best to Peter--I hope his individual creative impulse is thriving--and of course love to my little Anna, I named her for my mother.

(But why women want to bring children into this world before certain things are straightened out, I can't see.)

Best wishes for the happiness of you all--

April 14, 1942

My dear Mrs. Lee:

I think Gordon felt my hand rather heavy upon him when I refused to let him keep a dog in the Fellowship. But probably it was not the dog entirely.

We had a talk about it but I didn't get clear just what was troubling him. We were all surprised and we were disappointed because we were all fond of Gordon.

He has talent and gave a good account of himself in the Fellowship.

He is now in Washington (west coast), I believe.

You need not worry about him. He is in very good health and he will get on, I am sure.

March 1-3, 1943

Dear Gordon [Lee]:

Such a nice letter from such a fine boy. I've said of you that you were "the only apprentice who ever left me for a dog." But while I know of course that was only the excuse I have never really known why you left, because you, probably, did not want to hurt my feelings too much.

I gather from the warm note just at hand, that I am a whiz in my work but as a private citizen I leave just as much to be desired now as when you left? Since I don't know just what you thought I lacked then, that doesn't hurt me too much.

We all make errors of judgement, if we have any judgement, and being a young fellow you ought to acquire a collection of errors in your own name as I have in mine.

But this is true--if you feel inclined, and opportunity offers, you are welcome to come back and we will take you in where you left off--as though nothing had happened at Taliesin to interrupt your work with us. This is entirely up to you.

June 20, 1950
Mr. C. Gordon Lee
Denver, Colorado

Dear Gordon:

   We are always glad to hear from Gordon. When you want to build a
house--let us know and we'll give you one to build.

May 12, 1943
Betty Mock
The Museum of Modern Art, New York

Dear Betty:

   I feel about "the best" work of art as I do about trees. There is no
"best"--only works of art.
   And any building in which I would be interested would be a work of
art. So there is no "best" as there is no best tree in the forest.
   My best to the two former Taliesinites--name of Mock--or is there
another? If so, that one too.

November 6, 1943
Iovanna Lloyd Wright
New York, N.Y.

   *Iovanna, Mr. and Mrs. Wright's youngest daughter, attended private
school in New York, at Madame Germaine Mariani's. While in New York
she also studied harp with Marcel Gandjany, the eminent concert harpist
who later spent a summer at Taliesin, teaching Iovanna and performing
for the Fellowship in Sunday evening concerts.*

Dearest Daughter:

   Such a nice letter! Seems you are quite content and "very please" wiz
ze Madame Mariani's place.
   I hope the master of the harp is inspiring you to play freely and not in
too academic style. I liked his quiet mastery very much.
   I guess you are out of money now so herewith is just a little. We are
keeping up money with the Madam. I think she won't complain.

Your hills and valleys are still a little greener here and there and the weather is not cold--the barn is framed and ready for the roof--the whole outside Taliesin woodwork is stained brown and all the window sash are bright but soft red. The studio is settled nicely again and I am at work in it. Mother has had the periodical relapses but not so severe as before. We must expect them for some time to come she says.

Svetlana "expects" again and Taliesin will soon look like a baby farm as well as a "fruit" farm, a dairy farm and a dirt farm.

They race around the studio at tea and are better than any circus. But Lord! how much care they are. And no doubt some of them will be terrific in time. All are showoffs. I guess they'll all be actors and actresses--not just as Shakespeare said it either--"all the world's a stage, etc."

Uncle Vlado's advice is good. He should take some of it himself. I hope you see Aunt Sophie often and I hope Aunt Maginel keeps up a kind of interest in you in spite of Nicky and that you are invited out to break the monotony of lessons and practice occasionally. I hear you are studying a little with Carol Robinson--"harmony" is it? Or something like that. She should be competent. How inspiring I don't know. Women seldom inspire women. But Carol is stronger than most women. Maybe she will. *[Carol Robinson, a friend of Mrs. Wright's from their days together at the Gurdjieff Institute at Fontainbleau, was a gifted concert pianist living in New York City.]*

The museum site is lost again and we are looking up another. Johnson's Wax wants to plan another building to build after the war. Celotex wants to see me "in two weeks" etc. so we are like to be busy enough. At last the studio is warm and I hope to finish the alterations to the old pig pen so it will be a good music-practice pavilion and small concert room.

Kenn writes an amazingly good letter. We are planning to go to camp in December. Kenn got out there on a motorcycle. Scared in the mountains--found lots of machines motors and metal things stolen--and the grounds full of steers and sheep, the canvas badly stained. Otherwise all as usual. He is putting things to rights but reports the cost of living there frightful. Inflation is here now. (He picked up another motorcyclist on the way out and kept him on at the camp.) We will fare better than most probably, on account of the farms--and post-war planning--so don't worry.

And don't worry about Mother. We'll take care of her and when she comes out of this she'll be much happier because better in every way. Those headaches of yours should grow less as you grow older--you know. You say nothing about them.

Because we lost the museum site I don't know when I'll be down again. Travel is vile--expensive and down to the mob level for the mob. You believe not in Democracy but in Mobocracy when you get about now--on the streets and in trains.

Have you heard from Howard Myers? *[Editor of the* Architectural
Forum *who was responsible for the two special issues devoted to Mr.
Wright's work: January 1938 and January 1948.]* Why not call up Mary?
Call up the Baroness and go to see the exhibition in the Gallery on 54th
Street--you know where. You might do her some good. She's desperate.
*[The Baroness Hilla von Rebay was curator for the Solomon R. Gug-
genheim Foundation collection of paintings. It was the Baroness who first
wrote to Mr. Wright in June of 1943 to ask him to design a museum for
Non-objective paintings, a collection which featured Wassily Kandinsky
and Rudolph Bauer.]* Go to good plays occasionally if there are any. Occasionally there is one. Read good things. (You might even read your
own Daddy's autobiography you know.) Don't feel you have to be on the
go all the time like the crowd in the streets. Be able to sit quiet once in a
while.

I'm glad you had a nice time with Marilyn. Tell her brother your father
never wore a label, political or religious, and won't now, not even "Isola-
tionist." Labels are all false these days and I guess they always were.

Roosevelt has sold his country down the river. We'll have to get it
back somehow...you and I.

I hope your finger came out all right but you "ring up" something like
that and then "hang up" and we don't know the rest. Nicky is a pest,
naturally enough. The Japanese have a proverb: "The very stones by the
wayside hate a boy under eleven." And I guess human nature is just the
same in New York as in Tokio?

Take the old "French business" as a tart and lick it off your fingers
when the time comes.

Taliesin is a great place and a great hope. So are you. We all look forward to what you are going to get out of this experience. It ought to add
much to Taliesin's charm and usefulness.

Here's your own daddy's love and a kiss, and wish for his daughter's
happiness--and usefulness to herself. And here's Daddy----at Taliesin.

February 8, 1944
Eric Lloyd Wright
Los Angeles, California

*Eric Lloyd Wright is the son of Mr. Wright's eldest son, Lloyd. Lloyd
practiced architecture in Los Angeles where he worked with his father on
the concrete block houses from 1920-25. During Mr. Wright's several
trips to Tokyo, Lloyd was put in charge of the work going on both for the
textile block houses (Millard, Ennis, Freeman, and Storer) and the projects
for Aline Barnsdall at Olive Hill. At the time of the following letter, Eric*

was still a young boy. Later he came to join the Fellowship and remained
for several years. He is now an architect residing in Malibu, California.

Dear Eric:

It's a great thing for a boy to have a Grandfather. And it's a great thing
too for a Father to have a Grandson.

So Grandfather Lloyd Wright is inviting Grandson Eric to spend next
summer vacation at Taliesin...where there are ancestral fields and hills
and weeds and horses...quaint old rigs..and pigs..and statues and paintings and a harp and grand pianos and draughting boards and a theatre
and dining tables and kitchens and chickens and ducks and geese...a
great herd of dairy cows..and beef cattle and a wide river to swim in with
great sand bars to play on where everybody makes music and
drawings...read and write poetry and stories.

Seems to Grandfather you would fit in to all of it and have fun and
work hard and play the flute with Aunt IOVANNA'S harp and sing with
the choir and all that...And Grandmother Olgivanna would be good to
you...

What do you say...grandson?

February 10, 1944

Dear Curtis *[Besinger]:*

Thanks for the Christmas drawing. The drawing was creditable to you
but my feeling about the building, admirable as it was, is that it was not
suited to your landscape there in Colorado.

We are creatively active. Very. We miss you here and will do anything
possible to get you back where you belong and I am sure you want to
be.

October 21, 1955

To whom it may concern:

During the past seventeen years or more Curtis Besinger has been in
close contact with myself in the building of some several hundred
buildings. He has had an experience therefore that any college professor

might envy and any professional architect would regard as paramount were there any realistic basis for such appraisal.

I am happy to recommend him for the faithful competent service he has rendered, not in connection with paper, but by actual experience in design to construction.

March 15, 1944
Betty Mock
The Museum of Modern Art, New York

Dear Betty Mock:

I hate to say this to you--but since your last Bettyfication, as I've been thinking the matter over--it appears to me that the exhibition of the Museum of Modern Art places me in a kind of competition. All entries-- either master, disciple, or exploiter are being held down to three exhibits for each competitor.

Thus, being the Era of the Shopkeeper, I suppose that this ruling is to give the boys an even break.

But whatever it may be no master feels it to be either complimentary or just. Always averse to sporadic exhibition of my work at all times dur- ing my life, I find myself unable to change in such circumstances as the Museum sets up. So I must insist that my work be kindly omitted from the competitive exhibition which the Museum of Modern Art has in- stituted.

It is of a kind with which I have never voluntarily cooperated, if you will remember.

August 28, 1944
Yen Liang
Yunnan, China

Dear Yen:

You were always a favorite at Taliesin. We expected you back some day, with your wife. We are happy that the day has come and will do all we can to help you across. I will find out just what steps are necessary in your case and take them.

Sunday evening concert in the Taliesin living room, Mr. and Mrs. Wright, Iovanna, and Svetlana surrounded by members of the Fellowship   1937

Taliesin chamber ensemble
Cabaret-theatre Taliesin West 1957

Birthday party in the Taliesin living room   1936

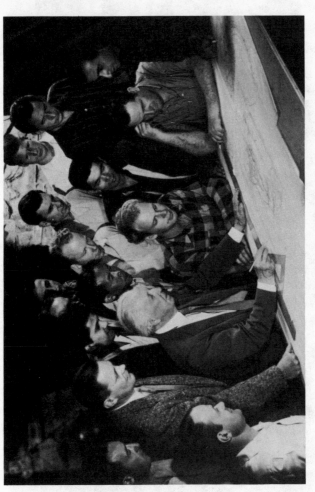

Hillside drafting room 1955

Seated left to right: John Howe, Frank Lloyd Wright, Eric Lloyd Wright, Wesley Peters. Standing left to right: Mark Hyman, Eugene Masselink, Raja Aederi, Ling Po, James Pfefferkorn, Alan Wool, David Dodge, Thomas Casey, Stephen Oyakawa, Donald Brown, Kenneth Lockhart, John Amarantides.

November 15, 1944
Iovanna Lloyd Wright
New York City, New York

Dear Daughter:

I am glad you miss me--else it would be just too bad to miss you the way I do.

San Francisco was quite fun. They made a lot out "of me and on me" too because the big hall for "the talk" was so full of people that we couldn't get into it when we came and still there was a queue extending each side the entrance door clear down and around the block. They said they turned over a thousand people away. The Pauson sisters were with me and they said "everyone in S.F. that mattered" was there. So see?

Mary Waterstreet has grown up remarkably--has a column in the S.F. Chronicle, broadcasts every noon and seems well liked by everyone. Good old Mary? Who could believe it?

Lots of people called up for houses and they worked me in for seven meetings in three days. Fred Langhorst was also a hero. Went out from Chicago on the City of S.F. Streamliner. Left S.F. on the Lark for L.A. The Chinese Consul's daughter--a lovely young person--wanted to come to Taliesin and she may. She went with me to the S. F. station to see about coming here. Saw Lloyd and Anne [Baxter, Mr. Wright's granddaughter] and Catherine. Went to see Anne rehearsing with Tallulah Bankhead--some Viennese play called, I think The...well, after all, I can't remember. Very dressy and sexy and elaborate, directed by Pressinger, the Viennese director whom I met and--etc., etc. Eric is getting bigger and sleepier. Slept all Sunday evening in his party clothes on the couch at Anne's--eats a lot of course as he's growing. Your sister Catherine is building a new house in S. F. designed by Lloyd himself.

Stopped at Phoenix two days to get the Camp lined up for us again. Left Hiram there as custodian to carry on. I guess he will--poor fellow. I sort of feel sorry for him as he is starting in on Architecture so late in life. He is a problem too....

I am enclosing money to buy a one-way ticket home. Get a reservation now if you can get one on a good train--it needn't be an extra fare train because time-saving isn't your main motive. We are celebrating Thanksgiving on Thursday, November 30th--the traditional one naturally.

Bring the harp--as we took it--checked on your ticket. And you would better take the Pennsylvania road because then you will be right at the Chicago station you go out of for Spring Green.

Quite a few people will be here so you would better prepare ten or fifteen things to play with your accustomed brilliance and "aplomb".

Our music drags along. The boys' choir is down to six. Svet hasn't much time to practice, Cornelia is picking up the cello a little. Why can't you "you all" down there find us one? should like to know?

The Baroness wrote a despondent letter and may have hanged herself by now. But I hope not. Poor Baroness! Go and see her but don't tell her about any work but the [Guggenheim] Museum. See? We are hard at work on that opus.

Well--my best love and we are one and all looking forward to a real Christmas of a time on Thanksgiving. Plan to stay as long as you like.

August 3, 1946
Edgar Allen Tafel
New York City, New York

Dear Edgar:

Go ahead with your project when you are ready. We will cooperate.
It was nice to see that little Tafel Boy back here where his home was for so many years.

December 31, 1946

Dear Steve [Oyakawa]:

Olgivanna and I and all the Fellowship send greetings and thanks for the sugar and everything you sent to us. We had very little until yours came. And how does your situation there please you?

[Stephen Oyakawa, at Taliesin from 1946 to 1961, was from Hawaii. During the war years he and his family frequently sent fruit and sugar to the Fellowship.]

January 3, 1947

Dear Aaron [Green]:

Nuts to the Fellowship from you are nevertheless a treat--thanks from us!
I suppose you have reformed Hollywood by now--

October 5, 1948

To whom it may concern:

   Aaron Green was an apprentice in architecture under my direction in the Taliesin Fellowship for a period of several years. He gave a very satisfactory account of himself in all the phases of our work which included actual building construction, draughting, and superintendence.

January 3, 1947
Mr. and Mrs. Kenneth Lockhart

   Kenn Lockhart came to Taliesin in 1939, and was sent by Mr. Wright to supervise the buildings at Florida Southern College for several years. Florida Southern is the one complete college campus designed by Frank Lloyd Wright who held that it represents the first truly "American" college campus built in this country.

Dear Kenn and Polly:

   The Fellowship will get real use from the excellent thermos container- miss you both on the picnics also.
   And thank you for sending the (you know what).
   We all were glad to hear of the theatrical advent of another Lockhart...

January 2, 1948
Edgar J. Kaufmann, Jr.
The Museum of Modern Art, New York

Dear Edgar:

   The perennial "fruit in season" is a real gift for us--thank you--

June 13, 1948

Dear Peter and Cornelia *[Berndtson]*:

What a birthday present and what a surprise! It must represent a real sacrifice on your part and a very fine thought. A good piece of work besides. I've needed something like this plan-case for years.

As Christmas time approached during one of the early years of the Fellowship, the apprentices came to Mrs. Wright to ask her advice about what they could give to Mr. Wright for a Christmas present. Money was scarce. Instead of buying something "ready made," Mrs. Wright suggested they make drawings of their own design, put them in a special box of their own making, and present them to him for Christmas. That suggestion became a tradition that has been going on to this day. "The Box," at Christmas and on his birthday, June 8th, provided Mr. Wright with the valuable chance to see into the artistic and architectural work of his apprentices on their own imaginative terms. If someone failed to contribute to "The Box," Mr. Wright was justly upset with the student. He placed great emphasis on this event, and his remarks on the projects presented were the greatest architectural "critiques" any apprentice would ever receive.

June 13, 1946

Dear Will and Virginia and Bob:

You have knocked us all quite silly--
The contributions to the Box astonished us all. You will be glad to see how they compare with the others.
Bob would be in danger of being considered a genius if that dream of his ever came true.

June 13, 1948

Dear Boys: Charles *[Montooth]*, Richard *[Salter]*, Paolo *[Soleri]*, Verne *[Rouillard]*, Mark *[Mills]*, Betty *[Mock]*, Ling Po, Fritzlie *[Betty's son]*:

Contributions to box duly received and admired. I hope all is harmonious and considerate. You will have my reactions to your drawings soon.

Carry on and remember Uncle Vlado is responsible to me for your actions where camp life is concerned.

N.B. Betty and Fritzlie..your special contribution was the sweetest one of all--

July 3, 1948

Dear Boys:

A few progress photographs of the minor desert opus would be good to see right now. Who could take them...Betty Mock?

Your box contributions are duly in place and appreciated. Paolo really went to town on his and all were surprisingly good.

Richard's quiet and characteristic--

Mark's an improvement on his previous performances--

Verne's scheme impressed me as most quietly architectural of them all--

Charles astonished me and was a credit to him. He is learning to draw--

Paolo's passionate rendering had a painter's virtuosity and technique, I thought. The plateau he mounted his well conceived building scheme upon was richly decorated by his buildings. But again they seemed to me all *on* the plateau, not *of* it. And there again even in scheme Paolo seemed more the brilliant *painter* than the *Architect*. But there are many roads to Architecture and he may find one of them if he is patient enough.

The chief purpose of the box, of course, is to acquaint me with what is characteristic of the contributors--where they are; of what they are thinking, etc. I have a peek in your direction by way of what you do--and that's all.

It must be getting warm now and I hear you work before sun-up. Charles gave me good reports of your working but of morale I am not so sure though he said everything was all right.

I have left Uncle Vlado in charge of Taliesin West to administer its affairs with your good and willing help. I hope all is harmonious and well. If you want to go to town on Wednesday as usual Uncle Vlado will give you the Model A but any other use of the affair or abuse is up to him. He is a good fellow and sensible and so far as I know he likes you all.

Mark is most familiar with the region and can show you around best.

My best to Betty Mock and Fritzli--and of course to you all--workers loyal to each other and loyal to your cause, probably *our* cause.

"L.H.S." are the initials of Louis Henri Sullivan, for whom Mr. Wright worked for nearly seven years. On his own time he was taking commissions for houses in and around Oak Park to help meet the needs of his growing family. Sullivan regarded this as a breach of their contract, and fired him. But towards the end of Sullivan's life Mr. Wright came back to help him. Sullivan had become a very sick man, down and out, living alone in a solitary room in a small hotel. Mr. Wright wrote often to him, visited him whenever he was in Chicago, and gave him financial help when he could. He had been called simply "Wright" during the time he worked in the firm of Adler and Sullivan, but in these later years an affectionate bond grew very strongly between the two, and Sullivan called him "Frank." Before his death, he gave Mr. Wright his last collection of original sketches and said: "You will be writing about these someday, Frank." Mr. Wright promised Sullivan he would. In 1948 he wrote the book, Genius and the Mobocracy.

December 1, 1948

Dear _____:

You are a bit mixed--I don't know what I might have been were I an apprentice to L.H.S. and therefore on intimate terms with him. Were you hired by me paid and fired by me for "independent" action you might be in a different case--more like mine with him.

I had no liberty of action with L.H.S. I didn't steal. Had he given me what you have had with me do you think he would have ruined me. I would have saved at least ten years of my architectural life but my whole life would then be different. So why speculate. You apparently never were an apprentice and should have been hired from the start--coming in and punching the clock at nine and going out at five--and probably fired long ago. "Independence" is not an aim in itself.

Apprenticeship is a cooperate state of being...sacrificial on both sides and so not for you. For intimacy here with my work you have no gratitude nor any understanding. What the boys here give or get or why-- or even what you got you wouldn't know. I am sorry but I didn't make you choose me. And I wouldn't break you because you did so like a fool instead of a man. You are free now as you ever have been, so far as I am concerned. Let's see what you would do if you were "independent" as you say.

You are entirely so--no longer a member of the Taliesin Fellowship. Evidently you made an error in coming here as an apprentice and should have been hired from the start.

DECEMBER 28, 1948
ALDEN B. DOW
MIDLAND, MICHIGAN

DEAR ALDEN:

DELAYED REPLY HOPING TO SAY YES TO GLAD CELEBRATION OF
YOUR NOW OFFICIAL STATUS FINISH ANOTHER BOTTLE SCOTCH BUT
HOUSTON MARCH FIFTEENTH AND INASMUCH DO NOT FLY DETROIT
TOO FAR. MEET YOU IN HOUSTON. THE OLD ORDER CHANGES BUT
THE HARVEST SHALL NOT BE YET.

June 4, 1949

Dear Iovanna...

Nice letter from Chamonix. So glad you are having memorable experiences in the old old world.

An evening or so ago I sat down to play our piano for a few minutes.
When I stopped and stood up a singing tone like a human cry persisted in
the air and for some moments. Astonished (and curious) I sat down to
play again. Again when I got up came the singing cry. Again I tried with
the same results.

Then I looked at your harp standing nearby and thought it must be
vibrating in unison with the piano. Again I tried and again the same song.

Then last night I had a vivid dream...

I heard something going on at the entrance to the Loggia. I got up to
see Gene pulling down a screen between the stone piers to conceal
someone in the Entry I thought. Mother was standing there trying to look
unconcerned.

I said, "Gene, what in the world is going on here". He said, "O,
nothing at all, Mr. Wright"...but at that moment you came out sideways
from the screen and came toward me saying, "hello Daddy"--put your
arms around me and kissed me--and I said "but you aren't really IOVAN-
NA are you. You are so little" (you felt so little in my arms). You said, "Oh
yes, I am Daddy". Mother said, "Why Frank. Of course it is Iovanna." And
you came and hugged me again and I saw you had grown more slight--
were not so tall as I remembered you and you had come all the way
home to surprise me. Then, just when I realized that you really were my
little daughter I woke up.

Your room is beautiful now but the white birch seems struggling for
leaves at the top. I will trim it. The house is very clean and in nice order. I
love it in the morning at sunrise best. The farm is getting itself together--

but we need a herdsman and a farmer and gardener. Perhaps you could find them in France or Switzerland--some family or two wanting to emigrate to our country. Bring them over with you.

Our work-folk around here aren't the right temper and anyway there is nobody fit to trust. If we can get good interested help we will go on very well from now on, I believe.

Anyway best love to you and the same great hope undiminished. Give my best to Jean Saltzman and Georgivanovitch, we send some nuts--

[In February, 1949, Iovanna went to Paris to study philosophy and dance correlation with her mother's teacher, Georgivanovitch Gurdjieff. When she returned to Taliesin in October of the same year, she started teaching classes of the Gurdjieff Movements to interested members of the Fellowship. This eventually led to her creative work in dance-dramas, performed annually for several years in the Pavilion at Taliesin West. Called the Taliesin Festival of Music and Dance, all participation—dance, drama, set designs, costumes, lighting, stage craft—was by the apprentices. Only the musicians were hired, mostly from the Phoenix Symphony Orchestra, to play the music composed for each dance-drama by Mrs. Wright.]

June 15, 1949

Dear Herbert *[Fritz]*:

Thank the Fritzes one and all for their share in "Opus 80 F.Ll.W." *[his 80th birthday]*. The quartet was a real treat. I had never heard Opus 130 before.

July 29, 1949

Dear Irene *[Buitenkant]*:

Along with the others you miss the bus. You start your piece as though there was a crew taking the initial ride. No. Not so.

L.H.S. and I began an era. Alone. There was no one else. Get that inside your little bonnet straight for a start and you may do some good to help rid the cause of the hoi-polloi--and get down the right basis. Who has done no more than use what they already found done. Some do better; some do worse.

I am still waiting to see the principles strike root and can only see the effects varied a little--a little to the left, a little to the right..Corbusier, Gropius, etc., etc., etc. No. Don't start me with a crew. I had a head start and the crew that came along after has only yet partially realized what it all really meant.

August 23, 1949
Charles Montooth
Spring Green, Wisconsin

Electricity at Taliesin West was originally generated by our own diesel plant, and apprentice Charles Montooth was subsequently assigned the job of installing a new system with its component wiring. Charles stayed at Taliesin over the years, and is one of our staff architects. When he married, he first practiced in Scottsdale, but came back to Taliesin with his wife, Minerva, who is now Mrs. Wright's secretary. Their two daughters, Susan and Margaret, are also on the staff.

Dear Charles:

I telephoned Sheppard to see if I couldn't get some credit for the cracked head of Diesel--but they said it was clearly carelessness in operation--lack of water that caused it and saw no reason for making any concession. So check to pay for carelessness is on the way. Who is to blame I cannot know. It seems all our trouble with Diesels comes not so much from lack of mechanical knowledge as faithful attention to oil, water and purifiers where needed.

We like you and don't look with pleasure upon your leaving at this time. John Crider is marrying--tomorrow--a nice girl (here from Canada this summer) and we are sending them to camp to stay until we come. So you could show John what to do and he would probably do it.

If you stuck around there probably some dark haired beauty would come and marry you. Not so likely back home--

Whatever you decided, good luck, Charles, and good faith usually gets it in God's good time--

July 12, 1949

Thank you Charles, for the contribution to the box and glad to hear the baby diesel is cutting down costs.

Best to all you Fuzzy Wuzzys at your 'ome in the Sudan.

April 12, 1950

Dear Charles:

We of the Foundation as well as we of the Fellowship regard your character and services as of true value to our work and would be glad to welcome you to our midst whenever the spirit moves.

See if you can't wangle a Crosley Hotshot from the Parental Authority as a souvenir of home at Taliesin.

January 25, 1950

Dear George and Helen *[Beal]*:

The Christmas pears were a treat--thank you for your thought sending them to us to link you up with our holidays.

January 9, 1952

Dear Ernest *[Brooks]*:

Ernest Brooks was a composer and pianist who took an active part in the Taliesin music-life during the early years of the Fellowship.

A pleasant surprise to hear from you after all these years. The music is a contribution to our library and the boys are working on it.

We all wish you a Happy New Year!

September 18, 1952

Dear Edgar *[Kaufmann]*:

We, all of us, have appropriate occasion now to work on a memorial to the beautiful woman who was your good mother. It would seem to be the chapel?

You--her son--are a grown man now and what she would expect of you is what your friends expect. Father is in a harder case.

Olgivanna and I are sure you are sure of our affectionate sympathy for we share your loss. Your mother needs no sympathy. She shines the brighter now that she no longer suffers. You and your father are the ones to receive whatever help we can give.

N.B. Seems to me the Mexico exhibit might be a good diversion at this time but I have so far heard nothing from them.

Eric Lloyd Wright was at Taliesin from 1948 to 1956, but during the Korean War he was in the Medical Corps. Previously, he spent the winter at Taliesin on the farm with John de Koven Hill, Kenn and Polly Lockhart.

October 15, 1952

Dear Eric *[Lloyd Wright]:*

I've read your letters, moved each time to write and have been each time moved away. ·

To the awakened mind all is grist to be ground. Keep at the grinding, Eric.

We all miss you more than we can say. You are a bright star in Taliesin's firmament. It is doubly gratifying when one's own bloodstream turns out a real help and filial friend. You have been that to us. And we follow your footsteps in alien territory, solicitous, with great confidence and affection.

January 3, 1953

Dear Fred and Maryanne *[Leibhart]:*

Well designed pottery. Fits in Taliesin West. Happy New Year to you both.

September 14, 1953

Dear Eric *[Lloyd Wright]:*

Let's say a great eternal spirit got Architecture born again when Louis Sullivan happened to get me, or I him. Let's say that the Taliesin Fellowship saw it on its way to grow up to man size fulfillment by that Fellowship's own faith and loyalty. Let's say that the Taliesin Fellowship is composed of individuals each with that single motivation come alive again as the basic element in our modern culture now missing for some five hundred years.

Let's say that each member inherits a trust to do with individuality what he may do, backed up by an establishment affording relief from financial worry, prestige of a great work and a great name, each individual free to carry on in this great background as he is able to do. Leadership then would have a latitude, a range, and a power lacking in the casual free for all. Yes. Well, that is my plan for Taliesin Next.

Every trained boy giving his life service to Taliesin has that certified insured establishment back of him to add to his effectiveness in the field of Architecture. The day when Architecture rides and rules again comes then--much closer than if it were left to the willful scatter of a rabble horde of self-seekers. Yes.

Well, the way progress is to be had and maintained is something like that, I believe, and have put my all into it the best way I know. Freedom of association in unity of purpose with a background of ordinance and ammunition.

Leadership. Who knows. That is something to be won, to be demonstrated and held democratic wise, so I believe. Why worry about that in advance of the great Idea. To serve the great Idea as a manly man is the basis of creative endeavor on the part of any individual. For him there is always more room for greater achievement than he, unsupported, uninspired, could ever hope to achieve. Civilization proves this. Democracy has banked upon it. By declaring the freedom of the individual, as such, Individuality was never regarded as personality but as the quality of the one desired and striven for by all--not vice versa. Everyman for himself and the devil for the hindmost was not regarded by its promulgators as Democracy. No. Do not mislead yourself or be misled.

The richer the soil (background) from which the individual to rise from, the better his chance of being beneficient to his fellows--as a creative individual. The finer the strain of character behind him, the better the chance of his superior contribution to society. Superior contribution to society is what Democracy asks of the Individual. If the Individual is too personal--throws away his natural advantages and wants to dot the I either prematurely or pretentiously Democracy has a liability not an asset in that person. See Eric. In union there is strength if there is really union. If there is not there is only confusion that comes from every man for himself only. Well, we will talk about it.

Love, (and Love is the spark plug of it all)

October 4, 1954
Dr. Moh'd Amin Khalil
Minia el Gamh, Egypt

My dear Dr. Khalil:

Your son is giving a very good account of himself in the Taliesin Fellowship. He is proving an industrious capable worker. I have spoken to him about writing to you. He says he will.

I congratulate you on having a fine son.

[Kamal Amin, from Cairo, Egypt, arrived in the Fellowship in January, 1951. He remained—except for a brief period in California—until 1977, when he opened up his own architectural-engineering practice in Scottsdale, Arizona. Kamal is a frequent guest at Taliesin, a constant reminder to those of us who know him well that he never really "left".]

November 4, 1954

Dear Aaron *[Green]*:

The very good apricots "am all gone, suh".

Your good letter contents noted. Better hang on to Oboler for a fee and to help.

Give my best to all the folks--

N.B. Damn Politics. *[This refers to the controversy concerning the restaurant Mr. Wright designed for Yosemite National Park. Politicians complained that Mr. Wright's design would be a "competing" attraction in the Park, and the committee was forced to select another architect.]*

December 24, 1955

My dear Curtis *[Besinger]*:

This is a little souvenir of appreciation and affection I should have been able to give you when you left but wasn't.

So--better late than never and a full and happy season to the ex-Taliesinist--

Whenever Mr. Wright was asked to exhibit his work in conjunction with other architects he replied that he did not..."wish to be hung out on the line with the others." Elizabeth Mock wrote to him asking to publish some of his houses along with works of other architects in a book she was editing. His reply, a propos of her request, was simply the "text" of one of his very favorite stories.

August 22, 1955

Dear Betty...

Little redhead (Susie) back of the room in Sunday school--
Teacher, "All you little children that want to go to heaven, raise your hands".
All but Susie.
Teacher, shocked, "Why, Susie, don't you want to go to heaven?"
Susie, "No, I don't, not if that crowd's a-goin'."

March 27, 1956
Andrew Devane
Baily Co., Dublin

Dear Andy:

Taliesin still remembers and loves the handsome talented genial young Irishman with the fine blue eyes and black hair. How happy we would all be to have you and your beautiful wife pay us a visit sometime.

Meantime, may your own genius inspire and keep you as a blessing to your time and place.

September 10, 1956
Allan Gelbin
New York City, New York

Allan Gelbin was in the Fellowship from 1949 to 1953. The following years he supervised several of Mr. Wright's houses in Ohio, New York and Connecticut.

Dear Allan:

Get well. Never mind the unnecessary strain. The thing will come out all right.

October 28, 1956
Edgar Kaufmann, Jr.
New York

Dear Edgar:

I am sure you know that I didn't mean to spoil your party--but for the second time in my life I broke in public--first at Lloyd Lewis' memorial meeting and this time at the beloved master's *[Louis Sullivan's]* post mortem.

Here was the A.I.A. that with their flags flying let him die, no help, sitting next me, etc., etc. Well, Edgar, I saw him die a squalid, miserable death and I didn't want to weep on the occasion in which I found myself, so I swore, my way.

A wrong note certainly because I could have contributed so much and I hope I did no harm to anyone but me and the A.I.A.

December 11, 1956
Mr. Henry Dreyfuss
South Pasadena, California

Dear Henry:

It is sad but true--all my Japanese friends a dozen of them young and old are all dead. Only one remains--a young architect named Taro Amano (in care of The Shokokusha Publishing Co., Inc., 12-2 Chome, Hirakawa-cho, Chiyoda-ku, Tokyo). Note to him enclosed.

January 21, 1957

Dear Marya [Lilien]:

Marya this Christmas was good Marya--

July 30, 1957
Robert Keeler Mosher
Malaga, Spain

Robert Mosher is one of the "Charter Members". He joined the Fellowship in 1932 and stayed for ten years. He helped in the supervision of both Fallingwater and the Johnson Wax Administration Building, and now practices architecture in Spain.

Dear Bobus:

We were all glad to hear you are well and happy and--as always--hard at work with enthusiasm. Enthusiasm, Bobbie, is your long suit. Don't lose it!

December, 1958
Mr. and Mrs. Aaron Green
Los Altos, California

Merry Christmas to the Greens and the Pausons in all time to come.

V

THE FINGERS ON MY HAND

Architectural drawing–drafting–is a most essential function of the Taliesin apprenticeship training in the field of architecture. In the first years of the Fellowship, when commissions were scarce, drafting was done on the buildings that existed at Taliesin and at Hillside to remodel them for the Fellowship and its new activities, including the design of special furniture. Many apprentices, in their spare moments following afternoon tea or the evening dinner, came back into the drafting room to trace or copy from the great wealth of drawings at their disposal–Mr. Wright's own renderings and sketches. Under his careful guidance we learned the craft of drafting and the art of drawing. His own ability, along the lines of architectural drafting, was expert in every way: he was a superb draftsman and justly demanded an excellent degree of fine draw-ing from all who worked for him or with him. His own "Lieber Meister", Louis H. Sullivan, recognized his gift for drawing when the 18 year old Frank Lloyd Wright applied for a job in the office of Adler and Sullivan. He prepared and brought some drawings to show to Mr. Sullivan. The famous architect, who was not given to compliment what was to him a mere draftsman, said, "Wright, you have a good touch...and you'll do." Soon the young aspiring architect-to-be was put in charge of the design department and given an office of his own, next to Louis Sullivan's.

Escalated way beyond his years, and above his peers, no longer the status of a mere draftsman, he achieved and earned this acknowledge-ment from Louis Sullivan not only because of his ability to draw swiftly and accurately, but also because he possessed a quick understanding of what his Master was trying to say in the language of sketches, designs, and ornament.

Having undergone such training under Sullivan, Mr. Wright would, as a matter of course, expect much of a draftsman, and later in his life, of an apprentice.

He referred to us as "the fingers on my hand", but every drawing we worked on was, of course, totally his. He was constantly in control of the whole; we were but the parts. He missed not one detail with his incredibly quick eye.

When the volume of his work increased over the years after the Fellowship first opened in 1932, the apprentices took on more responsibility in the drafting room in the making of perspectives and presentation drawings as well as the necessary working drawings. Mr. Wright explained to us the particular view or angle he wished to show the client, frequently making a thumbnail sketch on the preliminary studies to demonstrate how the final perspective should look. The mechanical projection of the lines from plan and elevation to third dimensional view was done by us. But at that stage of the drawing, he came into the drafting room, sat down and rendered it with colored pencils, erasing, adding, shading, making certain lines stronger, contrasting with other more delicate ones. Transforming an accurately made but otherwise dry and lifeless work, he breathed exquisite life into it.

He proceeded to teach his apprentices how they, themselves, should render with pencils and colored pencils, sepia ink, or India ink—there was a large choice of media. But no matter how skilled and expert an apprentice might become trying to perfect the drawing into finished form, whatever final touches Mr. Wright added and corrected, whether in lengthy detail or a few quick, decisive strokes, projected the quality of that drawing from the level of good work by a competent draftsman into a great work by an incomparable master.

Many of his letters contain instructions and remarks to his apprentices about the architectural work going on. Beginning with the model of the prophetic Broadacre City, and continuing with the famous Fallingwater at Bear Run, soon the Usonian Homes were conceived and construction of them started throughout the country. There is a decided break in the architectural work during the Second World War, but the commission and the designs for the Guggenheim Museum occurred at that time. The Guggenheim Museum and Marin County represent large works that were constructed, but there were projects that never left paper: Lenkurt Electric, the Masieri Memorial, and the Point View Residences among them.

On each work, large or small, he paid careful attention to each and every detail. His awareness of the client's budget was always present. Architecture, he fully realized, was the profession of getting a building built for someone at a cost he could afford. The following letters focus on the Fellowship at work, on the architecture of Frank Lloyd Wright.

September 21, 1933
Frederick Langhorst
Elgin, Illinois

Dear Fred:

   This is tardy acknowledgment of good work done on the Millard com-
panion piece. I was glad to have it and the group is gratifying now. What
University department could show as result of first year project--as much
sweetness and light with perfect sanity?
   We are preparing for the trek to the sojourn in Arizona. We miss you
very much and I, especially, believe your place is here. I wish we had a
scholarship for you.

   *In 1933, during his stay in the Taliesin Fellowship, Alden Dow made a
film of the Fellowship life. This film remains in our archives as a record of
those early years. It was shown in London in 1939, and has since been incorporated into documentaries both in the United States and abroad.*
   *The Arizona camp, at the time of this letter, was at the Hacienda Inn,
in Chandler, where the Fellowship set up living and working quarters to
make the models of Broadacre City.*

January 4, 1934
Vada and Alden Dow
Midland, Michigan

My dear Dows:

   Your thought for us took effect as you may imagine, both apples and
magazines. The apples are by now built into the Fellowship--the
magazines will keep us informed and disgusted with the fallacies and
vagaries of the passing capitalistic show. As antidote, we are engaged at
present upon an exciting project for a travelling highway-show of our
own [Broadacres] organized to set up its own shelter and unfold its
wonders within anywhere within a normal circusing radius of 2000 miles.
In this manner we hope to extend the good will and intentions of an
organic architecture for the United States where farmers, cooks, and
capitalists can see what the damned thing means if they are curious. I
guess they are or will be when the turnout turns up. For this we are to
have a 16mm. projector to show the film Alden began and that Vada
says we are, sometime, to have a print from--synchronized as before suggested with records made by myself--all to be delivered to small but frequent audiences along the highways and byways of our great and

glorious free land. The show is then as modern a circumstance as a
travelling butcher show would be. It will resemble somewhat the
Arizona camp and requires only a campus vacant urban lot for a host or a
sponsor. Posters we are designing will precede its advent. Pamphlets will
litter the precincts when it leaves. This much as a sign of the times. Mean-
while my affection. The Fellowship, such as it is, will testify to its own
gratification at your hands.

*Broadacre City was a design concept of city planning that came as a
prophetic revolution fifty years ago and is only now being understood, in
part, as those early seeds are slowly taking root today. It was conceived
as a city that was really not a city in the conventional sense. It placed
man, in his various civic and private needs, upon the landscape and in
harmony with it. It abolished the idea of massive centralization for a well-
planned decentralization.*

*Mr. Wright wrote the concepts of Broadacre City first in 1932 in a
book called* The Disappearing City. *Later a revised text was published
under the title* When Democracy Builds *and finally revised once again
and with additional drawings in 1958 as* The Living City.

*What he planned as a decentralized way of living in harmony with the
natural features of the land was intended, in 1934, as a solution that
would offer man a life of beauty combined with the necessities of work,
education, social and cultural activities. Many of Broadacre City's important features are coming into being today in a desperate need simply to
survive the brutalizing conditions of urban life.*

*In 1934, at a period in Taliesin's history when there was little architec-
tural work going on, Mr. Wright set about to construct a large model of
Broadacre City along with other supplementary models to show bridges,
traffic control, housing and services. During the winter of 1934-35 the
Fellowship migrated to Arizona and rented living and working space at
The Hacienda in Chandler. There, and mostly out-of-doors in the mild
winter sun, they constructed the models. Edgar Kaufmann, for whom
Fallingwater would be built, was a patron of the project.*

*The exhibition of the models opened in Pittsburgh and traveled
around the country, including Radio City in New York and the Corcoran
Gallery in Washington.*

December 3, 1934
William Beye Fyfe
Berlin, Connecticut

Dear Will Beye:

I don't imagine you'll be farming much until next Spring. So if your work is done and you care to return to work with us on the big model of Broadacres--12'0 square--we would like to have you. Owing to help we are getting on it I could pay you $30.00 to come on with and give you $20.00 per month, the several months you would be here--and some money to get back where you want to go.

I've written Bob Bishop likewise to come on for a couple of months if he has nothing to keep him away just now. Better wire if we may expect you as we need help.

December 3, 1934
Bob Bishop
Swarthmore, Pa.

My dear Bob:

Your second letter gave me pause. I don't like to ask you to give up a possible chance to get the help your parents need. I can't pay you enough outside your transport here and back again to make your sojourn of two months very helpful--say $40.00. This sum and including transportation would make your participation rather expensive where we were concerned although a sacrifice for you. Then too--I feel I should be looking for help where the center of gravity of the individual can lie within the future of the Fellowship.

I am a little tired of breaking in colts to harness at my plough and when they can pull a little letting them go to pull some other plough. Nothing at all in that, at my time of life or at any time. So that is changing as fast as I can change it. I've been careless about this hitherto but should now be less so. There is something I now want to build for the future.

The plan has changed entirely since your time aiming now more and more at organic simplicity. What that means exactly in the conduct of our activity here is coming clearer in pattern as we go along.

I am however enclosing $30.00 to pay your way to Taliesin if you really care to come to help us with the big model. We would be glad of your help because we know it would be competent and rendered in a fine spirit.

May 5, 1947

To Whom It May Concern:

Robert F. Bishop was an apprentice in the Taliesin Fellowship under my direction from 1932 to 1935. He has ability and a good character.

March 14, 1935
Mr. Alden Dow
Midland, Michigan

Dear Alden:

Here's to M. Lloyd Dow. And a swell name it is. Illustrious performances flock about the ring of it--not to mention me.

And I have long neglected the recognition of your helpful spirit--somehow, because I am sure of your understanding. A nice thing that two-fifty, Alden. You will get something back before long.

To Vada the young mother my hat is in my hand--a *son*--as I hoped. No doubt she is doing better than well because that is just what "happy" is.

I have taken your advice and got a number of jobs not to mention the magnum opus, Broadacres, which grows into something very beautiful and, we all hope and believe, something useful. You'll see it at Radio City which it is capable of blowing up into thin air.

It is now, between us, family to family. We wish you were with us in work as in spirit, but destiny's tracks seemed to go off to Michigan and you followed keen on the scent.

Come back and see us early next summer and bring the boy. You will all be always sure of a warm welcome at battered up old Taliesin.

April 28, 1935
Edgar A. Tafel
New York, N.Y.

Dear Edgar:

I've been rushing about since I returned, lecturing, etc.--and neglected your letter. The $200.00 was creative at that end and immediately went to work at this end.

It is all right to go to Washington or do anything either of you can do to promote our mutual stake in the Taliesin Fellowship. Use your own judgement in such matters when you can not get a response from me. This Washington matter looks a bit undignified again. A side show in a vestibule made and sponsored by ourselves only. Can't we go into the Corcoran Art Gallery or some place to which we might look for, at least, an invitation and some credit?

I am getting restive concerning the show. We need you boys and we need the truck. The dump truck we have acquired is going all the time on road and dam work. Can't we pull out there shortly after the 1st without raising animosity too high?

What importance do you attach to this desire to give me an official job? I am not inclined to take it too seriously. Were there something tangible in prospect I might come down.

Have yet had no word from Tom Maloney.

Tell Bob [Mosher] I appreciated his letter and saw his forebears at Cranbrook--a pleasant overflow occasion. Mr. Booth, the founder, was quite flabbergasted--had never seen the like at Cranbrook and began talking about building a big hall. Another job for Saarinen who was very nice. The Pavilion had 460 chairs for 650 people and several hundred had to be turned away unable to get into the place.

I appreciate your folks' kindness to Bob, of which he speaks in his letter.

Spring is here and beautiful as ever. We need you both at home. We are again caught short handed and late with our work. This year we won't have such a big garden so we can easily take care of it.

My best to you both, relatives and collaterals also.

Cornelia Brierly worked with Mr. Wright on the designs and construction of the Broadacre City model while the Fellowship was in winter residence in Chandler, Arizona. When the model travelled throughout the country, Mr. Wright sent Cornelia along with the exhibition to act as guide to the models and to explain the new concepts proposed by Broadacre City.

July 12, 1935
Mrs. Franklin D. Roosevelt
The White House
Washington, D.C.

My dear Madame President:

Across the lawn from your home, in the Corcoran Gallery, is a thoughtful presentation of an idea concerning the situation we face in our country at this time and that you would probably go to see if you knew what the idea really was or might mean at this time to our country. Hearsay is untrustworthy where this is concerned.

The gist of the idea presented there in the form of architectural models is not Utopian nor is it any ism or istic but seeks merely to sensibly interpret certain changes taking place in us and around us to find for them some way out of chaos.

It is hopeless to mend or modify what is already doomed. And I've never been much interested in reform. We need organic form and we are not going to get it until modern life is seen as a whole for better or for worse and some rational use is made of immense resources that are now stalemate or going to waste. We have the power in our hands to create anew if we would use it.

Were the models in some gallery in Europe I should not have to write a letter to ask my Queen or my King to see it. To them it would be prophetic and so indispensible. I would be better known to them than I am to you because "no prophet is with honor in his own country"--(you see how modest I am) and so in my own country I ask my madame President (and could I expect my President himself to see it?) to see the work.

I should like to explain the scheme myself but Miss Brierly, a Taliesin Fellowship girl, is there all the time the gallery is open and would be only too glad to try to make the plan come clear to you. Perhaps never before with any valid claim to being a work of art has a cross section of a whole civilization been made visible in every detail.

This work is there so near to you that I wonder if I might hope you would find time to see it for yourself for what it is worth before it comes home here July twenty first?

Respectfully yours,

Edgar J. Kaufmann first met Mr. Wright in 1934 as a result of his son, Edgar, Jr., joining the Fellowship. After he sponsored the construction of the Broadacre City models, he asked for a home on a site of falling cascades of water several miles outside of Pittsburgh. Fallingwater, the home of Mr. and Mrs. Edgar Kaufmann, on Bear Run, Pennsylvania, was the first large commission to come into the office after the Fellowship was started.

With the working drawings under way by spring of 1936, Mr. Wright sent Bob Mosher to start supervision of the construction.

June 12, 1936
Bob Mosher
Kaufman's Fifth Avenue, Pittsburgh, Pa.

Dear Bob:

Go ahead with the layout in relation to the original bench mark on hearth boulder and let the other boulders come where they will.
I have examined the plans and see no harm ahead.
The hearth can be got all right--the boulder can be cut for the boiler flue--the boiler itself being moved inward.
Water in the trenches will do no harm as a solidly made dry wall on stone ledge in the water is as good as a cement one.
But there should be no excess in the thirty-six feet. The slightly altered position of the stairway is unimportant. Let it stand.

N.B. There would be no objection to adding nine inches to the width of the kitchen and bedroom unit, if the boulder happens to make a bad contact or incidence with it. Better survey this and send elevations and dimensions. Your plan tells nothing.

Following the work on Fallingwater and the Johnson Wax Building, Mr. Wright designed a luxury residence for Herbert Johnson, himself, called "Wingspread." He was simultaneously at work on a new concept for moderate cost housing which he called the Usonian House. The project had its beginning in a residence proposed for South Dakota and another for Kansas both of these unexecuted. But in the house he designed for Herbert Jacobs the idea first took tangible form and was built in Madison, Wisconsin.
It was revolutionary in all aspects: the floor slab was a concrete mat set upon a crushed rock bed, in which were laid pipes for gravity heating. The masonry walls were the main supporting members, with board and batten sandwich wood walls treated as non-bearing screens, both outside and inside. The flat roofs were three-tiered, constructed of 2x4 framing throughout. A utility core housed kitchen and bath, laundry and heating facilities, centralizing them to conserve costs of piping and plumbing. Interior furnishings were designed as part of the whole, organic in character. Once the Jacobs house was completed in 1937, the Usonian House became a standard solution for this budget of housing that would be practical, buildable, and beautiful. Several of these were built throughout the United States.
The task of the Fellowship in its work on these new houses was twofold: first the making of the working drawings for a system of con-

struction that had never existed in architecture before; second the means of getting the houses built.

The typical general contractor did not understand the system of construction, nor the revolutionary concepts of building techniques they conveyed. Mr. Wright therefore would send one of his apprentices to the site, expenses paid by the client, to act as general contractor, interpret the plans, hire the various trades necessary–masonry, carpentry, plumbing, electrical–and to supervise construction.

This act of learning how to supervise a building designed by Frank 'Lloyd Wright could be difficult and painful, both for Mr. Wright and for the apprentice. Where he was not able to instruct them in person, he wrote in detail to explain the roles of architect, client, and apprentice, as in the following letters to John Lautner re the Roberts house and then the Sturges house–while the projects also claimed his attention.

June 16, 1936
John Lautner
Marquette, Michigan

My dear John:

You may be learning a lot about contracting--I don't know it. But you never learned much (or else you have forgotten) what is due an architect, or what being an architect means in these circumstances in which you now find yourself. I am at a loss to account for the rapidity with which you seem to have dropped all responsibility in that connection and shifted your center of gravity.

I am completely in the dark as to what is going on in connection with our work at Marquette and am beginning to suspect it was indiscreet to entrust the Superintendence of a Taliesin project to the son-in-law of a client, even when that son-in-law is you and Mrs. Roberts is the client. I have not had occasion in the several years you have been alongside to find you either faithless or dumb. But your conduct in the circumstances with this trust I have placed in you, seems to me both and is in sharp contrast to the conduct of Bob, who is in Pittsburgh with the Kaufmann house, or any similar trust I can recall.

Bob might lose his head and so lose his connection too, were it a family affair with him--I don't know.

At any rate he is aware of the need of keeping me daily intelligently aware of the work in progress--keeping up his reports and keeping in touch step by step fortunately for all concerned as frequently transpires.

Bob is there on the job because I had made arrangements with Kaufmann for one of the Taliesin boys as a clerk of the works for his keep and $25.00 per week, paid to the Fellowship. No such thing is included in any Architects "Superintendence" unless on that basis. But that is precisely what you are taking the liberty of handing (at Fellowship expense) to Mrs. Roberts, is it not?

I am willing to put a clerk of the works on the Roberts house if Mrs. Roberts is willing to pay for one as Mr. Kaufmann does. She should be willing and no doubt would be if necessary.

If you prefer to join the contractor in the building of this house, I will send one of the fellowship boys up to represent me as clerk of the works. Let the contractor put you on his pay-roll if you desire to resign your Fellowship.

I think I made it clear to you and to Mrs. Roberts that I wanted to join with her in making this building a good thing for you, but certainly not in taking a chance on having a building I have designed go on in the dark in unexperienced hands, completely helpless to defend myself against what I know from experience is sure to happen to it unless I am constantly in touch with Superintendence.

As I understand it, you went to Marquette for that purpose and none other.

There is no knowing in this office in the way of any record either of contract or any series of reports, or from completed plans concerning the Roberts house anything about it as things stand.

Mrs. Roberts doesn't care. She doesn't know anything about an architect's work. But you should know.

If you don't know you at least now have a chance to learn something about it from me. From now on, we begin.

July 15, 1936
John Lautner
Marquette, Michigan

Dear John:

Where is copy of Architect's contract?

Where are the daily reports of Superintendent to Architect?
Where is the tangible evidence of Fellowships in good standing:
                Mary Lautner--?
                John Lautner--?
Got tossed up in the air by the new grader. Net result--a couple of ribs pushed in--wrenched leg and neck. Hard to move about but disposition still sound.

Feel I ought to come up and will soon as possible.

Meantime, why not do your part in relation to us down here.

Love to all to whom love is due.

July 29, 1936
Robert K. Mosher
Kaufmann's Bear Run Camp, Penna.

Dear Bob:

I do not want to drop the terrace floor now affixed to the boulder. I
like very much its natural relation to the two upper stories. It does the
house harm to "level up" this terrace.
Senior Kaufmann's room can be as he wants it.
The window on the terrace side is only cut off and we have it as you
have guessed it except the bed in place of wardrobe. I see no objection
to that change if he likes it.
The concrete ribs however are part of the structural integrity of the
whole fabric and should go in as they are designed. They are working. I
have given a good deal of attention to the concrete structure as it stands
and do not want tile instead. Gypsum slabs are all right--strong enough,
light and cheap. No water gets to them anywhere and if it did the results
would not be serious.
The suggestion of slopping about at the entrance does not appeal to
me much. We will offer a substitute if the necessity really exists.

August 21, 1936
Robert K. Mosher
Kaufmann's Bear Run Camp, Penna.

Dear Bob:

In discussing matters with our client it is well to have in mind the
motif of the building--that is to say the reason why it is as it is where it is.
We got down into that glen to associate directly with the stream and
planned the house for that association. Hence the steps from living room
to stream. I intended to deepen the stream for a swimming pool under
the house at the foot of those steps. With artificial collateral pools we
look foolish.
Again the main floor is a projecting *balcony* over the stream. To put
stairs from the balcony to the ground robs the balcony of any character
or romance as such.
The stone work was intended to blend with that of the glen. But the
walls built before we got there do not. The later work on the big
chimney pier does so. Something must be done to the corner of the
bridge and collateral piers to change the scale. I can knock off stickouts

to help get the effect when I come down but we will have to set in a chunk or two here and there.

In view of our building as in the glen to associate with and play with the natural stream, it might be all right to dam the stream itself in some natural way in keeping with the rocks that are its boundary. Say just above the falls to make a ripple or two before the deep fall and so make the stream itself deep enough for a plunge under the house. If the water should rise high enough to cover the stone walls under the bolsters it would not offend me.

But I shouldn't like to see this ripple over two feet above the rocks that now precipitate the fall. Less would be better.

It seems to me there is already three or four feet of depth where the steps come down as the ledge now slopes in that direction. But if not some blasting could be done by someone who knows how, in order to make a deep enough pool. I should think, five feet ample for depth of water or perhaps four.

As for the stone bath tub in the entry, I suggest it be outside nearby where flowers can be thrown in it to keep them fresh and our clients can dip their feet without wetting the entry floor.

February 3, 1937
John E. Lautner
Marquette, Michigan

Dear John:

Have you yet found anyone to finish the house? I would like to know in detail what is happening up there. There is much to do down here, you know.

November 17, 1937
Edgar J. Kaufmann Jr.
Pittsburgh, Pennsylvania

Dear Edgar:

Rather tardy reply to query concerning table lamp. There is no reason why the thing shouldn't spin if you want to whirl it. Otherwise I can't see the advantage of more than a quarter or half turn. For the office we are making the wood key that fills the opening in the glass--also the wood handles for the doors.

Mrs. Saarinen is well on with the rugs and covers for the furniture. The chair is finished. We are sending it on with instructions regarding that god-awful upholstery. It was all wrong anyway and will have to be cut down and reshaped as indicated.

What about skin rugs? Or can we put in something more immediately available?

I hope Senior is not going to let us "die on the vine". I've heard nothing from him in reply to "the sorrowful" [the invoice] I sent him.

September 13, 1938
John E. Lautner Jr.
Los Angeles, California

Dear John:

We have been corresponding with Mr. Sturges (George D. Sturges, 1843 W. 30th Street, Los Angeles). He wants a Jacobs House and has sent in the requirements and a good sketch of the lot. We will send a preliminary which you may present to him for criticism and return it for final plan making. It will do no harm to have an authentic unit in the low cost housing field out there if it is well done. So, let's see how it will work out this time.

February 11, 1939
John Edward Lautner Junior
Hollywood, California

Dear John

Herewith sketches for the Sturges. I think it is self explanatory. Take it to them for their reaction.

It is one of the simplest things we have done and one of the best.

September 12, 1939
John Edward Lautner Jr.
Los Angeles, California

Dear John:

Will pay the $75.00 graft. Steel is nonsense and so are 6" instead of 4" beams. I wouldn't give a rap except in their eye for any science an L.A. Beaurocrat assesses. I guess Lloyd wasn't much help. I suggest you offer to build as designed and make test. If test not satisfactory then agree to add steel--flitches--to meet requirements.

Meantime the mill deck floors can be fir or whatever is easiest to get at a low price. The grade can be low as any edge grain shows in the building. It could be resawed--knots cut out as you go along--nailing the strips every 2'0. Timbers can be likewise and all boarding too. If "rough" too hard to maintain use surface dressed. If long timbers add too much to expense laminate them of l" x 12s. The edges could look nice--like plywood edges.

The roofs will be 4 ply tar and gravel with 3/4" Wearcote mixed on the job--on top. No counter flashings needed but mop up on walls and fix cap sheet strip as indicated on sections. Floor of Balcony excepted. The boarding on the big soffit of main overhang needs only the same lap as the walls and one thickness is enough. The lap is shown too heavy.

Fill in Chimney mass with loose rubble--using only shells with cross walls where flues occur.

Low grade brick--common o.k. Watch joints (50-50 lime and cement) and stain them afterward--red--approved treatment. Leave off special shoe at start of all partitions and walls inside and start with batten.

1. Hinge horizontal boards to give excess kitchen light--a technicality.

2. All sash should be white pine stained Cherokee red. Instead of loose-stops could be for putty.

3. 2x4s in floor O.K.--very low grade can be used (nailed).

4. Surfaced like floor and probably to save time and money all wood elsewhere the same.

5. Yes, but new cross-head screw with electric screw driver is almost as easy as the screw nails.

6. Sisalkraft will do but cheap tarred felt will do also. No flashings--see details.

7. 2x4s o.k. for concrete--will give horizontal grain which we can let alone for effect.

8. o.k.

9. Will make designs for hangings and furniture.

10. Mix your gravel in concrete mixer with reddish low grade concrete--and put over 2-1/2" thick. If washouts add more from time to time until stable.

9'0 projection of yard walls from main house wall is o.k. I pushed it out only to take advantage of level ground. What a survey!

Hardware should not run so high. Let's eliminate.

Wiring should not run over $150.00. Let's investigate.

Plumbing is too high.

Heating is too low.

Ought to beat lumber price $750 to $1000.00

Bricklayer should lay 600 bricks a day against concrete wall.

We got 350 to 500 pressed, raked and on curve in Johnson building. How many bricks to lay?

Roofing shouldn't cost over $150.00 if you do it yourself.

Glass o.k. (must be plate--absolutely--but can be *thin 1/8" plate*)

Carpentry--$1000.00--seems reasonable.

Where are sash and door items included?

A mill schedule should be made--at once and you would better make it.

The linotile can wait--omit partitions in the basement.

Concrete cost us $5.00 per cubic foot on the Johnson job with expensive metal forms.

Don't let the job drag--if you get held up lay off your men but don't get "held up".

Specifications seem to be in Arizona. Will send copies.

The brick grills in Foundation Wall under big overhang make walls look weak.

Make as shown in revision herewith.

September 15, 1939
Mr. A.G. Green
Florence, Alabama

Aaron Green was a practicing architect in Florence, Alabama, when Stanley Rosenbaum came to him for a house design. Aaron convinced Mr. Rosenbaum that if he went to Frank Lloyd Wright he would get the best. Mr. Wright suggested that Aaron, along with Burt Goodrich, supervise the work.

Mr. Wright subsequently invited Aaron to join the Taliesin Fellowship, where he stayed for many years until he enlisted during the war.

My dear Green:

I intended the sketches to be sent to you but by mistake here they went directly to Rosenbaum.

I hope you all like them. A nice house to live in down there?

October 6, 1939
Mr. John Edward Lautner
Los Angeles, California

Dear John:

In going over the foolish figures and details...I find the "Eng" has made the Sturges pay $435.00 for divorcing the structure from the design--and weakening the integrity of the building as a whole. *Exactly that.* It is a culpable outrage--what to do I don't know as I don't want to hold up the building--or do I?

The natural boarding and interlacing of the soffits where all the material that entered into actual structure added up a big factor of safety has been ignored really in ignorance of its actual nature. Artificial, expensive, foolish "corrections" are now employed really only to make Sturges pay for an Engineer and steel. There is apparently some concert between the Engr. and Dept. whereby both live on the home owner.

The added beams are only weight to be carried. The "tips" indicate that the Engineer is "balmy". The "code" is also made not for the house owner but for the material supply men.

I see not one sensible appreciation or any understanding of what *constitutes good construction*--that is to say--integral--in this senseless interference--so what? The "corrections" demanded are totally inferior to the interlacings and direct contact nailings which they ignore.

The building is now all cut up and cut off--hanging to a skeleton because the Engineer couldn't understand anything else. I suppose Lloyd is helpless and can do nothing. If I were on the ground I would start something to try and vindicate good construction as against out of date stock and shop framing and save my client's money. The Sturges must decide-- now.

September 21, 1939
Mr. A. G. Green
Florence, Alabama

My dear Green:

We have found it impossible to get the advantages of our simplifications (and extensions of space) into our client's hands by way of the present "contract" set-up. The clients are really "fixed" by the cash and carry system for departing from the channels laid down.

So we itemize all mill work--let contracts for piece work--brick per thousand laid and measured in the wall--concrete per cu. ft. laid, lumber according to our own bill, etc., etc.

This throws a strain on us incommensurate with an architect's fee and we meet it by sending on an apprentice at the proper time to take charge, do shopping and hold the whole together--checking all layouts, etc.

The owner is asked to lodge and feed him, pay his traveling expenses and pay to the Fellowship $25.00 per week for his services so long as required--(it should not be in this case longer than ten weeks). We have standardized details during the years we have been working on the modest priced house problem and feel that in this way we can not only save our clients most of the general contractor's fee but get results of which we can be proud.

When our clients are ready to proceed I suggest we proceed in this way.

N.B. There is no harm in getting local bids unless some local feeling aroused when we step into do the work--more or less--ourselves.

When the original set of presentation drawings (sometimes referred to by Mr. Wright as the sketches) were sent to the client, and received the client's approval, they were returned to Mr. Wright so that the working drawings could be started.

SEPTEMBER 29, 1939
A. G. GREEN
FLORENCE, ALABAMA

PLEASE ASK ROSENBAUM TO RETURN SKETCHES. WE ARE PROCEEDING WITH PLANS.

February 20, 1940
Mr. Burton J. Goodrich
Florence, Alabama

Dear Burt:

Rosenbaum is supposed by terms of agreement to pay the expenses of your trip there and back, to shelter and feed you only while you are necessary to his work there. $25.00 per week he should pay to the

Fellowship--that's me in such case--half to be retained by you--half sent to us. Has Rosenbaum done this? If so, I am willing to let up on him from February 15th forward, but we cannot afford to deduct a membership for more than eight or ten weeks to get one little house built, Burt.

Better get set up there so a subsequent visit or two will be sufficient. Rosenbaum is expected to pay expenses of such trips also.

No occasion for you to reduce your share in any event.

We will design the furniture here and submit sketches to him. It will all be much the same for the Usonian type house and can be made by Harris Mill in Chicago where we can inspect it.

FEBRUARY 28, 1940
BURTON J. GOODRICH
FLORENCE, ALABAMA

TELL ROSENBAUM WILLING YOU SHOULD STAY ANOTHER MONTH TO PUSH THINGS ALONG.

Mr. Wright was in constant contact with the apprentices who were on the sites supervising his buildings, and he steadfastly expected them to report to him at regular intervals. Frequently his notes and letters were brief, but sometimes they were more detailed as the occasion required. His telephone calls were famous for their brevity.

March 27, 1940
Burton Goodrich
Florence, Alabama

My dear Burt:

Send me as soon as you can progress photos of the Rosenbaum House and a complete breakdown of all the costs complete to date and in sight.

No news may be good news--maybe not?

March 31, 1940
John Lautner
Los Angeles, California

Dear John:

Have revised the plans, clearing up construction, putting on figures.
Lloyd made the analysis required once upon a time and it may serve.
You might ask him. Will be in L.A. next Friday morning. See you then.

April 24, 1940
Burton J. Goodrich
Florence, Alabama

Dear Burt:

Herewith answers to your questions:
1. Lighting: ceiling bulbs or above shelves or set into square recesses
in ceiling with sanded glass over.
2. "Sisalkraft" is o.k. for insulation. It is all right to tack Sisalkraft to
ceilings.
3. We will design easy chairs.
4. Get price from local mill for making all furniture--tables, etc.
5. Drawers and shelves o.k.
6. All furniture to be cypress same as house.
7. Wardrobe arrangement is o.k.
8. Upholstery to be blue Crochette (same material as in House at
Taliesin)
9. Rug arrangement is O.K.
We are en route to Wisconsin in a day or two--

December 31, 1941

TO WHOM IT MAY CONCERN:

Burton J. Goodrich was a member of the Taliesin Fellowship from
August 1934 to August 1941. He has proven himself to be a conscientious and a careful worker. He is capable of handling tools and turning
out a craftsmanlike job. He is a thorough and good draughtsman.
I am sure he will give good account of himself in whatever he undertakes to do.

Mr. Wright was open to suggestions of solutions to problems as they arose during construction. The Usonian House system was constantly being refined because of this ability of Mr. Wright's to continually improve on the original concept. But he was adamant that no circumstance, concession or comprise interfere with the idea of his work.

The text of the following letter, to one of the supervising apprentices for a client in California, vividly illustrates this concern. The situation had become a crisis and Mr. Wright was forced to deal with it in strong terms.

September 24, 1941

Dear John *[Lautner]*:

I learn (from you) with astonishment, plus chagrin, that _____ has put Aalto furniture into the opus I gave him! No greater proof of the fact that he doesn't really know what it is all about could he give me of his intelligence. The Aalto furniture is a tour de force in the first place--an unnatural use of wood to simulate steel springs and utterly unsuited to my buildings--a farce in fact.

The _____ opuses (I learn it with real pain) are evidently the proverbial pearl. I am deeply disappointed because I too like _____ and believed he had something. Where was John Lautner that he let such a thing happen. John must know better. *And* if _____ informs me correctly on his costs he is up against circumstances that take him, like a poor fool, for a ride. Costs are just about double what we are doing similar work for (not in such an out of the way place though) in 27 different states right now.

I don't know what to think. Perhaps I should just write the thing off as another one of those "Hollywood experiences" that I've heard plenty about from Lloyd and my friends and am to experience for myself. I fall in love with my houses and to bid them to the devil is hard.

What is it in the air out there? Our Midwest and Eastern clients are very different. They have great faith in us and are rewarded.

Out there if one of our houses leaks the world hears about it. Probably every architect in L.A. had houses with leaky roofs (if I am properly advised) but somehow what does it matter? I am a far better technician than any of them with ten times the experience. But it appears that my apprentice-system of superintendence needs some revision. It is getting it. If ever you encroached upon the nature of my office in relation to my work in the fashion that seems so prevalent out there I am sure to resent it in my own way. You wouldn't like it nor would anyone.

I will not permit _____ to build the main house without a clause in the contract that would protect the work from his own destructive tactics, or the tastes and ignorance of others, no matter who or when or how. Well, this is a bad moment your news gives me.

We will appear in L.A. before long and if you go through with
Stoneweb (alias Sijistan) we will look after it ourselves--in person. Hell,
there is no other way. Michelangelo, Beethoven, Bach, Brunelleschi
found that out. I hoped to overcome the handicap I suffer in comparison-
but the combination of client and builder plus the money matter is no
easy hurdle for the creative work to vanquish.
    We will see what we shall see--
    My best, meantime--
    Affection as always,

December 1, 1942

Dear John [Lautner]:

    _____ made more promises and we are waiting to see what
becomes of them--
    I understand they are about to wreck the Barnsdall House. We would
like to secure the bas-relief over the fireplace, some of the glass and
some of the sculpture. Would you see if we can get it from the man who
is doing the wrecking for the city?
    Love to Mary and the children--

*In the midst of much building construction in many states and more
projects on the drawing boards at Taliesin, the Second World War sud-
denly intervened. Shortage of building materials curtailed any architecture that was not directly related to the war effort. Taliesin lost many of
its apprentices to the various branches of the armed services. Others
were sent to CO camps, according to their religious convictions, and
three went to Sandstone Prison, in Minnesota, because they refused to
go into war but did not have the religious background that would make
them immune from imprisonment. Mr. Wright tried repeatedly to have
these deferred and sent back to Taliesin for work on the farmlands.*

March 28, 1941

    THE TALIESIN FELLOWSHIP was founded in 1932 near Spring Green,
Wisconsin, by Frank Lloyd Wright, American Architect, to accomplish the
following work herein stated:

We submit that we are associated in a task which may honestly be called a national objective:

1. To create upon the thousand acre farm and in the architectural workshops and the home buildings of Taliesin a way of life firmly based upon the American tradition of hard work and yet establish a convincing example of indigenous American culture.

2. To assist young men to develop their creative capacities on building better buildings for America, buildings more truly expressive of the land we live in and of the people of our great Democracy.

3. To train such builder-architects by continuous actual experience in planning and building with every kind of tool and material, first upon the farm and buildings of the Fellowship, later by work and superintendence upon important buildings now in actual construction by ourselves throughout the country. Necessarily the endeavor of the Taliesin Fellowship is upon a completely legal, non-profit basis known as the Frank Lloyd Wright Foundation.

4. To this end every resource within the power of its leader has gone to build up not only the internal strength of the Fellowship work-life but to get materials to work with and to extend the opportunities for the work and growth of the young men and women of the group. For the past eight years the energies and continual work of an average of twenty-seven worker-apprentices has gone into the Foundation. By the natural process of selection inevitable in the circumstances this group has been so knit together that it now stands well equipped to do the work it set out to do for our country.

To preserve for Americans what we must believe to be a true form of self-defense, we the undersigned members of the Taliesin Fellowship hereby go on record as objectors to Compulsory Military Draft which threatens not only to destroy us as a group but violates the deepest concern of our individual consciences.

To compel the breaking up of the consequences of these years of training is a far more serious loss to America at this time than the loss to the American army of men whose convictions, educations, and principles render them unfit for destruction and mass murder called war. Therefore we respectfully ask that we be allowed to work as a group for interior defense rather than be compelled to waste our lives in jail. We ask that our services in preparing for war be used in the constructive field in which we are already engaged in the effort to preserve American Democracy. Compulsory conscription will only scatter and render us impotent.

THE TALIESIN FELLOWSHIP

May 8, 1942
Dr. James Jackson
Madison, Wisconsin

Dear Dr. James Jackson:

I am at least grateful for your open and direct expression of feeling yesterday concerning myself, my work, and my helpers. It is better than the hypocrisy that sometimes passes for friendship or politeness. I came to discuss deferred employment for certain of my young men at Taliesin, but conscientious-objection came up. Why prejudice and insult persisted as you proceeded, I soon understood. I do not have to drink a tub of dye to know what color it is.

But both your prejudices and your insults were bared as based on falsehoods. Falsehoods which, I am now sure, you would not like to disbelieve.

Falsehood number one: you said that I banded the young men who are my student-apprentices together as conscientious objectors. Here is a list of members of the Taliesin Fellowship now in service:

Fredric Benedict: Army
James Charlton: Army
Benjamin Dombar: Army
C. Gordon Lee: Army
Gordon Chadwick: Army
Robert C. May: Army
Burton Goodrich: Marines
Charles Samson: Marines
Loch Crane: Flying Corps
Ed Whiting: Flying Corps
Peter Sanford: Navy
Blaine Drake: Defense Work
Peter Berndtson: Defense Work
Edgar Tafel: Defense Work
Ellis Jacobs: Defense Work
Rowan Maiden: Defense Work
Alfred Bush: Defense Work

Observe that seventeen out of a possible thirty-one are already in service and five more are given A-1 Classification. This practically wipes out the Taliesin Fellowship and our works. I am unaware of such destruction as this visited by conscription upon educational work in our country. There is undoubtedly an honest reason for this.

Since you have insulted the young men whose fate, as luck will have it, lies in your hands and instead of judging their case on its merits--you gratuitously charge them with dishonor as having no consciences of their own except as I dictate to them, and you said you were going to disregard them as grown-up men and citizens because of your feeling about them and about me and you were going to deal with them summarily as traitors to your own son: I think that then you put it squarely up to me to see that harm likely to come to them because of your personal prejudice founded on lies and bias does not deprive them of a free trial under a free judge.

I don't believe the laws of our country were designedly put into the hands of prejudiced men to administer. When it does sometimes happen, as it must, an appeal is provided for by law. And while these young men know where I stand and I have carefully refrained from influencing or advising them in any way as to their own acts up to this time, I feel that to save them from the consequences of such prejudice as you profess, I must, if I can, help them to appeal their case to a higher court. A court of justice.

June 26, 1942

Dear Bob [Mosher]:

Enclosed is worksheet on Model A. Seems rings should be all it needed. Crack in block is not serious as it can be sealed. It developed on the way back from L.A. A new block with all connections costs but $58.00 at Sears. Plus $15.00 for installation. So I fail to "get" the $125.00 charge for remodeling by Mesa. These repairs would have enabled you to be here quite comfortably by now. But probably Hand should have a car and Hunt will look in on him occasionally.

He is writing a book and feels the need of the "hot and dry" for his health. Solitude is no bar to his contentment. He promised faithfully to be here July 9th. He has a Pullman ticket to Phoenix. He gets $30.00 per month and expenses from then on.

The Fellowship boys who have left are all in the army except Edgar and Bob May. They may be safe outside the Fellowship but it doesn't look that way. I've had a timely run-in with the appeal board at Madison who reproached me with the fact that "the Taliesin registrants" have all had more than a year's exemption already on account of their fool C.O. stand. I expect they don't want to go to bat with that issue. You can read my letter to the chairman when you arrive. Looks too like a willful sending of the sheep to slaughter from now on. The English are washing up in the Middle East and that means no fighting chance.

Bring the Scott radio with you as baggage. There is no use leaving that there. We will be glad to see you back. We've all been more than unusually busy and constructive since we got back. Taliesin is more than ever beautiful this year.

My best to Aaron--poor devil. I am sorry he felt he had to run into arms. The Detroit group are all C.O.s and may haze him when he gets there.

November 30, 1942

Dear Burt [Goodrich]:

Your letter was welcome and reminded us of the Burt at Taliesin, only now he is a slave whereas at Taliesin he was free. But to maintain that kind of freedom he had to sacrifice himself and fight as he is to fight now. Only he chose his weapons then; the old infamy chooses the weapons for him now.

Why not go to Russia, Burt, and enlist and fight on the only front that seems to really matter since you have no faith in Taliesin's weapons? We often think and speak of you in the Fellowship. You were a pretty faithful Fellow for almost ten years and your young life during that period is well built-in, I hope, to what we call Taliesin. I wish it might stand you in good stead.

December 5, 1942

Dear Jim [Thomson]:

You are doing better. A nice roomy homey little house! We are glad of it.

So Mother is still with one of her chicks in spite of distance and circumstance. Give her our love. And we hope to hear your wings over Taliesin some day and look up to see you trumpeting up there in the sky.

Olgivanna is getting better; Iovanna is a young lady just seventeen; Svetlana is a mother and music-master now; Wes is a great farmer; Jack [Howe] still bullies the fellows in the draughting room; Gene is still drawing and typing and singing and laughing, etc., etc.

Most of the Fellowship would be new to you. War has taken (or scared away) nineteen and wants five more. That about folds us up.

We have shut down Hillside for the winter and with the big root cellar filled, what there is left of us expect to come forth in the spring with double chins--

June 2, 1943

This is to certify that John Howe, Allen Davison, John Hill, and Ted Bower have been and are essential to the all out farm effort of the Taliesin Farms. All are competent help having been trained in such service as well as in Architecture.

Even with these boys deferred for the necessary farmwork we are shorthanded. We need more help if our garden truck fruits, crops, and animal husbandry are going to produce what they should.

Since Architecture went out some time ago, farming about twelve hundred acres is our work at Taliesin.

August 26, 1943
Curtis Besinger
Mancos, Colorado

Curtis Bessinger came to Taliesin in 1939 and stayed until 1955. During the war years he was sent to a CO camp because his religious affiliation prohibited his going to war.

Dear Curtis:

For several weeks I have been hospitalized--but am able again. Your letter is amusing and indicates a morale unflagging. Sure--everything associated with character is meat for a growing architect.

Have you applied for parole to Taliesin as we expected you to do?

Political prisoners find executive clemency hard to get. Whatever they call you, you are really a political prisoner. We would like to hasten the process that gets you back here to us. We need you and hope you will let us know what we can do and when.

Don't allow frustration a foot-hold in your soul. You have not sinned-- not even against man. Keep your head high, your heart warm and your feet on good ground.

December 22, 1943

Dear Curtis:

I haven't had word from or of you for sometime and wonder how it all goes down with you now.

We are sending you our best with a good hope and in the same faith to which we have all subscribed--a better world to live in because it will reflect the great harmony in the Spirit of Man that we call Architecture.

It would be a great Christmas present to your Fellowship to have you with us. You have been a good number--as the slang goes--and we want your Fellowship to be "a good number" to you. We are back of you to any limit, Curtis--and with affection--

In principle Mr. Wright was opposed to war and to the United States being dragged into a European conflict. He was especially opposed to conscription. But regardless of what direction the war years took his apprentices, into the conflict itself, or into CO camps, or into prison, he always supported each in his own choice. Marcus Weston, Allen Davison ("Davy"), and John Howe were finally sent to prison.

May 14, 1941

Marcus Weston is the son of Will Weston, a remarkably skilled carpenter from Spring Green who assisted in the building of Taliesin. When Mr. and Mrs. Wright first moved to a desert camp at Chandler, Ocatilla, it was Will Weston who again supervised and built the wood and canvas structure that so quickly became famous around the world.

To whom it may concern:

I have known Marcus Weston all of his life and he has been associated with the Taliesin Fellowship for the past three years. I have found him intelligent, upright and extremely conscientious. He has a mind of his own and does his thinking for himself.

March 22, 1943
Marcus Weston
Federal Correctional Institution
Sandstone, Minnesota

Dear Marcus:

Hearing many good reports of the place we are all anxious to know how your garden is growing at Sandstone. We wanted to send up your unfinished model of the church so you could work on it. Your warden answered me asking for dimensions. I have given them to him. We expect to hear from him soon. I think you will like him.

Just recently I am back from Washington. Spent a couple of weeks there. Saw my friend Thurman Arnold and Attorney General Biddle. General Hershey too. [Robert] Sher was busy on your case with pretty good hope. You have probably heard from him now and then.

I don't believe the law or the United States really intends to persecute any man. But, prosecution does sometimes become persecution and this war is either going to go toward civilizing us or barbarizing us some more, which all goes to show that we, as a people, got freedom before we knew just how to use it for our own good.

The white blanket of zero weather is still here. Henning is a sheep farmer now. He got Dick's eighty. Davy is getting Robson's farm. So he is soon a farmer too. Wes takes Enos Jones' place and Gene will have a print-shop there. Wes will likely take on Hank Michel's place also in order to turn it over to somebody in the Fellowship someday. So we are moving toward Broadacre City.

A letter came this morning from a Miss Boss of Evanston who said she knew you. She is interested in coming to the Fellowship. She interviewed Jack's mother. Looks like Jack and Johnny and Davy and a few others will be deferred for farming. Your friend, H.B.I. Howard, told Gene that "Taliesin was now to get a break." I don't know what exactly or why it should be so late if it means anything. But legalities often move back and forth.

Your pals in the Fellowship all think and speak of you often hoping you will be back before too long a good deal better off for the wear and tear of taking it on the chin. You would sure fit in around here.

Lorentzen has refused a lawyer and is taking care of his own case, I believe.

Remember me kindly to your warden. I expect to drop in up there around the eighteenth of May to tell the boys why Architecture is more important to them than anything else because it is fundamentally structure.

April 27, 1943

Dear Marcus:

I've just received a letter from Sher in which he says he is trying to have you paroled to me here at Taliesin and that word should come through any day now. I wanted to await word from him before writing. I am talking at Eau Claire May 17th and expect to come up to Sandstone to talk to the boys there the next day or two. Will probably bring Olgivanna and the Willeys along.

Spring has been fighting its way in to join us and there is a tinge of green over the willows and the pastures are now quite green. All the spring birds are in the choir below the windows.

There are several new buddies on their way to join the Fellowship but we will be small in number this summer. We do not yet know if the local board will defer Davy and Jack as farm workers but the others seem fairly certain to be.

The war gives every evidence of being a long drawn out affair that can end only in defeat for everyone engaged in it--defeat of one sort or another. To "win the war" is only to lose heavily in every way. To lose it is no better. So what is ahead no man may say.

The tone of your letters shows a clear conscience at least. And so long as that is so your growth won't stop, your spirit will be clear and you'll not be too unhappy....It seems better to go to jail with your conscience clear than it is to stay out with a guilty one.

After all, nothing is more important than to be on good terms with one's self. One lives there and quiet faith in one's self at that point is an essential to any true happiness. The worst trials we sustain are the self inflicted sufferings of others because of us. But after all we can't live dependent upon what others think for us or about us. We have to be square with what's inside.

I guess you realize that more than ever now that you are confined to yourself and you must gain strength by the faith in yourself that comes from living up to your faith. I've had enough of it to realize there is nothing quite like it. You are at least false to no man when you are true to yourself. And you won't be true to any man when you are false to yourself.

Things at Taliesin are getting a thorough going over preparing for summer--changing and adding a little here and there where it makes a great difference.

Your father comes over to work occasionally. Wes and Svet aren't yet in their apartment but are nearly there.

Easter we ate breakfast together. The Baba and Pashka were unusually good. Johnny made the Pashka under Olgivanna's direction.

We all gave you a silent thought and a hope. Meantime we enjoy your letters at tea time.

It will be a great relief and a happy day for us when we see you with us again--

Affection from Olgivanna, Iovanna and myself in which the whole Fellowship enthusiastically joins--

N.B. Do you have your guitar with you? A good chance to add to your repertoire and also entertain your fellows at Sandstone?

April 27, 1943
G. W. Humphrey, Warden
Federal Correctional Institution
Sandstone, Minnesota

My dear Warden:

I am speaking to the Teachers College at Eau Claire May 17th and think I might get to Sandstone the day after that by way of Minneapolis. Dean Willey of the University of Minnesota and his wife and my wife, Olgivanna, will probably accompany me as they are interested in Marcus and Sandstone.

I am sending you a copy of the lectures I delivered in London some few years ago--what I shall say at Sandstone will follow the same direction. I may bring along some 16mm colored films--motion pictures showing our work here at Taliesin as well as houses we have built. I presume you have a 16mm movie projector?

In 1942 Mr. Wright designed a housing project for the Detroit auto workers, called berm houses. They were a revolutionary use of packed soil against a concrete wall, the soil then covered with mosses and grasses to help insulate the house both in summer and winter.

June 10, 1943

Dear Marcus:

Just back from Washington where I received confirmation from the Department of Justice of your parole not to a C. O. camp but to some approved work which you might choose for yourself. I put in a formal application to have you sent to Detroit to carry on your education working on the dirt-houses for the Detroit defense workers. But they said they were afraid of the controversey that might arise although the suggestion would receive consideration.

You seem to be headed for the West Coast meantime--a comparatively free man.

We would all like to see you before you leave. I am writing to the Warden to see if you could come along this way to see your folks on the way West. We will all be hearing from you and you from us at will. I imagine you are not quite at liberty.

Davy and Jack's case has been postponed in the hope that 2-C, deferring them for agriculture, will be coming through on Presidential appeal now being made.

December 18, 1943
An Open Letter to Patrick Stone from Frank Lloyd Wright

You do not know me. I know you only as you disgrace your judgeship to throw stones at me. The quality of American fair play is sunk pretty low when a judge uses his office (however he came by it) to sound off from his bench the prejudice he conceived against another man on mere hearsay.

And we have plenty of prejudice taking refuge under the name of government when it is to no more than a passing administration of government. I have occasion to know well the arrogant prejudice raised against any man who refuses to run with the pack, but it is seldom that it comes from the place all American citizens hoped to keep free and impartial.

So I believe you are another one of the things that is the matter with America. I think for the safety of the nation such men as yourself should be deprived of administrative authority right now.

In the case of Marcus Weston, a conscientious-objector, you tried him only as a draft-evader and sentenced him as a criminal because he knew no better than to plead guilty to the charge against him which was itself an evasion of his real status.

I have no more use for a draft-evader than you have.

The Taliesin Fellowship is a tax-free Democratic establishment wherein young men are recognized as responsible human beings with consciences. I would never take it upon myself to advise them what to do with their own lives--even were I consulted. It would not be in the spirit of our Fellowship.

But they are here because of a common interest and faith: I often learn more from them than they learn from me. It is not surprising therefore that their feeling about war should independently somewhat resemble mine. Independence is their status here as they will gladly testify because all are volunteers.

As for conscription I think it has deprived every young man in America of the honor and privilege of dedicating himself as a free man to the service of his country. He [Marcus] was first condemned without a hearing and enslaved. Were I born forty years later than 1869 I too should be a conscientious objector.

December 22, 1943

Dear Marcus:

A word of greeting this Christmas when the Christ spirit seems needed so much more than ever.

We don't hear much from you now from which we infer that you are easier in mind and circumstances. You were a faithful son of Taliesin and Taliesin got you to thinking. You won't be a paper hanger now.

And I hope you won't be less than helpful to the great cause your Fellowship committed you to whether you knew it or not--and that is making man's share in the Earth a true reflection of his great spirit.

So to you--Marcus--who sort of kinda grew up here around the place we all send our faith and our good hope for you.

And I have more than a mere personal interest in what you are and what you will do.

We all wish you were here with us and we look forward to seeing you restored to the growth and good work of our cause--which is a great one-- even if few understand it or value it.

Be good--if being good doesn't make you so lonesome you can't take it.

January 5, 1944
John H. Howe and Allen Davison
Sandstone, Minnesota

Dear Boys:

Your contributions to the annual Christmas box--this year a pig-skin portfolio by the Berndtsons--was a knock-out. The boys, owing to getting it ready for the portfolio, saw the drawings before I did.

My first reaction was, Well I guess Jail is no bar to the growth of im- agination. Fine renderings--boys--by the whole damn two of yez.

Davy is mastering color; Jack is mastering line. I should say Jack is sometimes too near the Ausgefurtebauten renderings but new effects coming through and is he prolific? Say! Jack has 'em like rabbits. The fan- tasy called the Airport is the best and a beautiful rendering I thought, but two of the collection of Usonians were daisies. I could build them just as they are--almost. Time at Taliesin made good by time at Sandstone.

Davy's idea of a house against the big bank was a whiz-bang of an idea. And what beautiful renderings. I didn't like the spider-like supports (too insistent and in the way) but did much admire the concept as a whole.

What a shame that such man-power as this is wasted while the na- tions quarrel like a pack of dogs over tweedle-dee and tweedle-dum-- mine or yours--this'n or that'n--which is mine? Etc., Etc. The radio sounds like a barker at a football game. Well, you see that quarreling comes in here where it has no place. And my boys have to go out where they do not belong for crimes they do not commit unless having a conscience is a crime. "They" make it one unless you agree to cut it and run with the pack. The "majority" is the "pack".

But make the most of it, boys. There is something about being in jail that affords a sense of peace and protection. Nothing can get you from the outside. The walls--as your drawings show--aren't there. You are where and as you will be.

And as soon as the politicians stop drafting men for the conference at the peace table we hope to see you where you count a rousing one for the future of the U.S.A. It has no future that war can advance. But you fellows have something it needs so badly that the need can't be hid much longer.

Thank you sons. Your work vindicates both yourself and me--

August 4, 1944
Mr. G. W. Humphrey, Warden
Sandstone, Minnesota

My dear Mr. Humphrey:

Allen Lape Davison and John Henry Howe come up for Parole sometime next September. Haven't these talented young men been punished enough? The wording of a congressional statute denied them a conscience as men, disgraced them and uprooted them for a year and a half. Is there anything to be gained by emphasizing that especial cruelty. If so will you kindly tell me what it is?

Further keeping them from an occupation so beneficial to their country as farming and contributing their work to models for postwar-living, a work for which they have been especially trained by years of experience, can serve no good purpose.

Allen Davison has a farm of his own, a wife and a child. Jack Howe has no family but is a most promising asset to his country as a young architect and farm worker. Both especially valuable to their country in the work they were taken away from to go into prison for the best years of their lives and are badly needed.

Can the best interests of such a country as ours be served by destroying them further? Have they not already been given enough to live down? In the light of postwar reason, such destruction by the administration of over-Government is going to look bad to us, I believe. What do you think?

Mercy extended in such circumstances, allowing these young men to once more pick up and try to mend the break in their lives by going on with their Life-work (especially when that Life-work is of so beneficient a public character at this time) would seem only desirable.

Would you suggest that I come up to speak to the parole board in this connection? Or what would you suggest that I might do to help in this sorry situation?

[Allen Davison (Davy) came to Taliesin in 1938, and became a member of the staff following Mr. Wright's death in 1959. Davy died at Taliesin West in 1974. According to his instructions a generous bequest from his estate has made possible the work done recently in filming Mr. Wright's drawings by the Frank Lloyd Wright Memorial Foundation.]

August 16, 1944

Dear Jack *[Howe]*:

I guess you know where I've been all this long time since I last wrote you--and (as Gene corresponds) how.

I've looked at your beautiful drawings with admiration, read your developing thought with hope and pleasure meantime doing what I could without rousing antagonism to further your release from punishment up there.

I've never needed my own "Fellows" so much as I need them now. And I know how much you Fellows need your Fellowship. My impotence in connection with your imprisonment is hard to bear. There is no possible appeal to Justice or to Reason. Only Prejudice runs with the pack and only a bigger Fear can have any effect upon its Fear.

But the Pack eventually tires and the consequences of its "running" when it stops to look back are undone. It will be so in your case. Your acts have been your own and you have taken it all on the chin and made the best of it like real men.

I can't even yet believe that faithful men and courage are not properly rewarded in kind, at least, even now. We will see what the next act in the serio-comic tragedy brings forth. The great thing for us all is not to lose faith in ourselves especially when our faith in others is lost.

We are necessitous here as never before. We have land to work; buildings to build; both activities way beyond our present capacity while you capables--trained to do it well--are kept there under the corrective lash so to speak, a kind of social debris. There must be some satisfaction somewhere? But what gain to Society?

Meantime be good. Let's see what happens.

August 20, 1945
Warden G. W. Humphrey
Sandstone, Minnesota

Dear Warden Humphrey:

It has been long since Mrs. Wright and I visited your work at Sandstone and we should like to come again. We could come during this week or next. Would this be convenient for you?

I should be glad to talk with you again. And, if you wish me to, to the boys--a short one--

October 9, 1945

Dear Curtis *[Besinger]:*

Don't be silly. We are devoted to you at Taliesin and wouldn't hear of your going anywhere else.

This is your spiritual as well as physical home, I should say.

You will have $30.00 per month in your pocket while you stay--and probably more later on. We will count your time in camp as Fellowship time and cut you in on the emoluments customary after the usual four year term.

Get your leg out of the goddam trap and report for duty without any more dubiety.

October 18, 1945

Dear Aaron *[Green]:*

Thanks for everything. I would like to see my old friends in Japan. Suppose you look up Arata Endo, Architect and Aisaku Hayashi, manager of the Imperial when the new one was built. Give them my best.

Time recently printed an account of the destruction and rebuilding of the hotel quoting me as saying "Let the Japs do it themselves". I am incapable of using the word "Japs" and I denied ever being asked to rebuild it.

Pass that along will you?

When do we see you in something constructive?

The moment the war terminated, architectural commissions began to come into the studio at Taliesin. In 1947, 32 commissions were on the boards, and ten years later, in 1957, there were 51. Not all of these were constructed, of course, but all required preliminary drawings, and a great many of them went into full working drawing stage. The unexecuted designs from these years–1945-1959–now comprise a vast wealth of architectural work to be built. It is our aim at Taliesin to see that it someday is.

May 22, 1945

Dear G. M. [Loeb]:

Mr. Wright designed a country estate for Mr. Loeb in Redding, Conn. which was not built.

Concerning your invitation to Ted.

Ted worked on your drawings to be sure. But he worked as other boys work at Taliesin, under my own hand reproducing what I have either done myself or initiated, and under daily, usually hourly, check.

He is yet a cub--and nothing you could do with him or he with you would equal a letter from you to me or one from me to you.

No Taliesin boy in training here has any relation to the client or should have. It would result in absurdity and confusion no end. There will be a number of boys at work on each plan, tracing and detailing, but no instructions or consultations with them could affect the results--or has.

This is not the usual condition in architect's offices but the buildings we turn out are not similar.

I dislike denying Ted a vacation but neither he nor we can afford one at this juncture.

Gesundheit...G. M.!--Angate--Sayonara!

The commission for the Solomon R. Guggenheim Museum came in June of 1943. Preliminary studies were prepared and signed by the following September, and by 1945 the set of working drawings was complete. Mr. Guggenheim, however, delayed the construction on the assumption that the United States was about to plunge into a depression following the end of the war, and the funds he set aside for his building would therefore go farther and build more. Mr. Wright warned him that the opposite would take place: building costs would continue to rise. They did. With many revisions, and several sets of working drawings having been drawn over the years, a final set was completed in 1956 and ap-

*proved by the codes of the City of New York. Construction began 7 years
after Mr. Guggenheim died, and 13 years after the original concept.*

March 18, 1947
Burton J. Goodrich
Portland, Oregon

Dear Burt:

   [Guggenheim] Museum model returned from New York completely
collapsed. Needs to be reglued. Can you arrange your affairs so to come
and direct the work. Bring your wife. Will pay all expenses self and wife
and five hundred dollars. Should not take more than a month at most. If
you need advance let me know.

June 27, 1947
Edgar A. Tafel
New York, N.Y.

Dear Edgar:

   Glad to see you anytime, but concerning the Co-op project--no
worry.
   If they like the idea I submitted we will work it out. If not it is all right
with me. We will work it out elsewhere.
   Plenty of opportunities waiting as *you* ought to know--

FEBRUARY 21, 1948
BENJAMIN DOMBAR
CINCINNATI, OHIO

   WOULD YOU BE INTERESTED OR ABLE TO UNDERTAKE
SUPERINTENDENCE OF EXTENSIVE ADDITION TO ROSENBAUM HOUSE,
FLORENCE, ALABAMA. FEE ORIGINAL PROVISION FOR APPRENTICE
PLUS TWO PERCENT ARCHITECT'S SUPERINTENDENCE FEE.

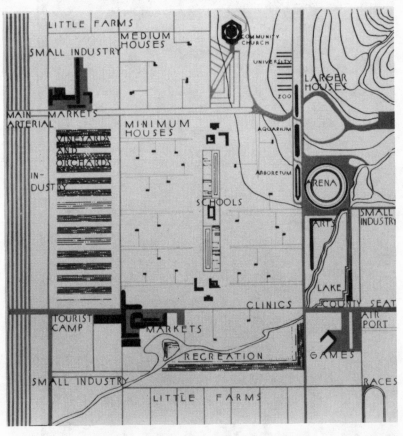

Broadacre City   schematic plan   1934

"Fallingwater" Edgar J. Kaufmann house
Bear Run, Pa.   1935

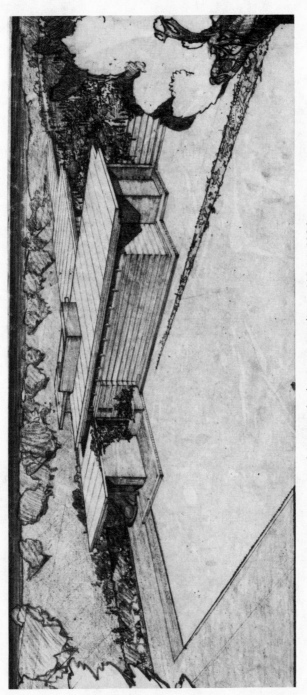

Herbert Jacobs house   Madison, Wis.   1936

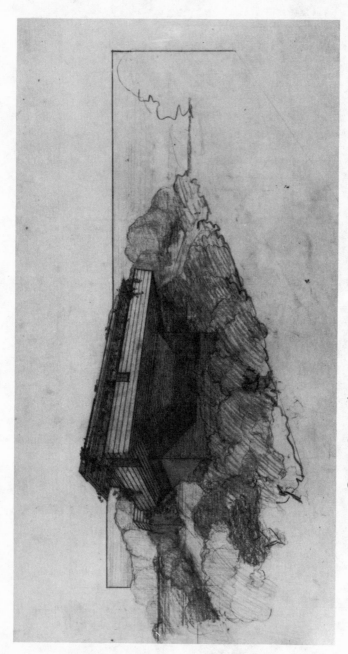

George Sturges house   Brentwood Heights, Ca.   1939

The Solomon R. Guggenheim Museum
New York, N.Y.   1943

Marin County Civic Center
San Raphael, Ca.   1957

March 20, 1948

Dear Rosenbaums:

Benjamin Dombar (988 Cleveland Avenue, Cincinnati, Ohio) now a young architect would like to superintend your house, he says, in response to a wire from me. Write to him and see what you think about it.

August 23, 1949

Dear Jack:

If you remember a talk with me on the eve of your departure. I told you you were not to consider your life as apart from the work going on at Taliesin but to come back fortnightly to report and receive correction if need be and instructions.

The client is expected to be willing to pay the expenses of these trips. There is nothing in the results obtained from your presence in the various fields to which I have sent you to warrant your ignoring this phase of your activity. You have now had a long time out and it is way past time to show up here with what you have in hand.

February 14, 1950

Dear Edgar *[Kaufmann, Jr.]*:

Have just seen your "piece" on the Morris Shop; find it quiet, dignified, and interesting. Your illustrations, too, are much better than Forum's. Thank you.

No word from Senior except a small check to pay off on the Garage at $20,000.00 or 1% instead of the 3% paid us by others. I believe you heard me refuse to make them for that price. I did refuse and take this maneuver as equivalent to being fired, although no word came along except a note from the controller's office saying "payment in full." Well, what do you say you would do in the circumstances.

I asked for the return of the Point Park studies as agreed in writing with Senior before I would send them but we can't seem to get them. Would you care to inquire into the why of the wherefore for us.

And I am terribly anxious to know about the state of my friend E.J.'s health. Please tell me.

December 21, 1950
Mr. Pedro Guerrero
New York

Dear Pete:

A most comprehensive exhibition of my work at the Strozzi Palace in Italy under auspices of the Italian Government is being assembled in Philadelphia and a preview is to be given there about January 25th. In May it goes on to its destination. Eventually it may go to India, Switzerland, Germany, France and England.

We have included several of your photographs already approved by us. Inasmuch as no "publication" is involved and some desirable publicity for you involved we have assumed your willing cooperation for which accept my thanks.

December 3, 1951
J. Clarence Davies Realty Company, Inc.
New York, N.Y.

Gentlemen:

Pedro E. Guerrero was a member of our Fellowship for about two years--1940, 1941. He is a good architectural photographer with good character.

FEBRUARY 12, 1951
DAVID T. HENKEN
PLEASANTVILLE, N.Y.

SKETCHES JUST ARRIVED. MAILING TODAY. GREETINGS TO ED.

FEBRUARY 13, 1951
ERIC LLOYD WRIGHT
SPRING GREEN, WISCONSIN

WHERE IS GROUND FLOOR PLAN LOUIS B. HALL. PLEASE AIRMAIL.
GREETINGS.

FEBRUARY 13, 1951
JOHN HILL
SPRING GREEN, WISCONSIN

PLEASE AIRMAIL ALL PLANS FOR BERM TYPE HOUSE IN STEEL
CABINET TO RIGHT UNDER WINDOW.

April 3, 1951

Dear John:

John deKoven Hill (Johnny) came to Taliesin in 1938.
He lived for a period of time in New York where he was the Editorial
Director of House Beautiful *magazine. He is Secretary of The Frank Lloyd*
Wright Foundation.

No power-line hookup. We are going ahead with the direct con-
nected generator system. Can get no concessions from the Wisconsin
Power and Light Company. They have confiscated our river.
Will have present generator systemed. Contact the Madison agent of
Harvester and report to him the conditions.
Where are the house plans I wired for.
Will suggest to Bob Cross that he take over when the time comes.
Carry on.

July 21, 1951
Appeals Board, HQ Continental Air Command
Mitchell AFB, New York

Tom Casey is on the staff at Taliesin. He works mostly in the engineering aspect of our firm's work but is a licensed architect as well.

Gentlemen:

We are writing in behalf of Edmund T. Casey who is now a member in good standing of The Frank Lloyd Wright Foundation. He is a student of Architecture under my direction.

Mr. Casey, a promising young architect, is in the second year of his work and studies with the Foundation. He has given excellent account of himself in all branches of his study and activity: in draughting, building-construction, design and engineering or on the farm. He is holding a responsible position as do all students at the Foundation.

The Frank Lloyd Wright Foundation is a non-profit accredited cultural-educational establishment incorporated under the laws and regulations of the State of Wisconsin, officially recognized by the United States Government and the Veterans Administration. Since the war some fifty veteran-trainees have preferred to take their architectural training at the Foundation where they are not confined to books or theory but actually experience Architecture at the source.

The Foundation has a group of seniors of the status of professors, a daily curriculum or plan of work, and if the student qualifies, a degree in the tangible form of a recommendation from Mr. Frank Lloyd Wright, President of the Foundation, which ensures him recognition and employment wherever Architecture is practiced as a profession.

We respectfully suggest that Mr. Casey be allowed to continue his good work with the Foundation.

August 17, 1951
W. Kelly Oliver
Englewood, Colorado

William Kelly Oliver was at Taliesin for seven years, and supervised the construction of the Gillin House in Dallas, and the Kalita Humphreys Theater of the Dallas Theater Center.

Dear Kelly:

Good to hear from you and to hear all is going as well as may be expected. We are all hard at work and especially upon the Unitarian Church right now.

Best wishes to you both--

August 28, 1951

Dear Vlado and Sophie:

We have been pretty much out of our customary world this summer and after the international hegira so gratifying and remarkable, I've been confined to the house for several weeks with what they call acute bronchitis.

Well, don't have it. That's all.

I hope things are not too bad with you. There must be bad times to appreciate good ones when they come. I thought I had settled the light problem for you before we left for Europe. I am trying now again by buying part way underground. I hope this will work. I can't see poles and wires along the highway and have started suit against the high-line authority. We will be out early this year, about the middle of November.

It is a great comfort to know that someone is in charge of the camp with our interest at heart--and hope you get something for yourselves out of it and out of Kelly Oliver.

I understand it is Sophie's turn to be sick so she can feel for me a little. I am as unaccustomed to it as she is. But that great invalid Vlado is so used to sickness that he wouldn't know when he was well. *[Mr. Wright is teasing Uncle Vlado, who was known for his robust good health.]*

I anticipate a pleasant winter session out there in spite of all our troubles all around...and enclose a hundred bucks for cigarettes, etc. Cheer up a little. It does no real harm to be sad and despondent because then things can brighten. If they are always bright then they can only be dark.

I hope now light will break for you. Charles left to court a girl in Phoenix. Do you ever see him?

David fell off the floor-slab. I guess he'll come "to" this fall when we get there.

You too.

It won't be long now, Vlado. The first hundred years is hardest and 'tho I've done more than you have, you have quite a score behind you.

And Sophie, we miss your quiet ways with whatever goes on around you.

"The Duke", too, is good company. I often wish he were around.

November 5, 1951
Benjamin Dombar
Cincinnati, Ohio

Dear Bennie:

Go to see Kraus at my expense and see if you can let his contracts to some one you know to good advantage.

January 1, 1952
Kenneth Lockhart
Spring Green, Wisconsin

Dear Kenn:

Herewith a very little wherewithal and a heartfelt hope for a good new year. We are still knocked to pieces at the camp making radical changes to incorporate glass, a new chimney, etc.,etc.

Money is going instead of coming but we expect to change that next February when I go to New York on the Guggenheim....

Anyhow, I know it's hard work and with Morton away you need help. So sell the pigs and get temporary help there if you can. Morton is coming back to stay. Eric should leave a week or so early so to spend some time here at the camp with us and go on to some little time with his pa and ma.

If you can manage it, would like you and Polly and the children to come here for a month (say March?) if we can find a temporary stopgap at the farm. Meantime we are all with you and hope for the best and...

January 18, 1952

Baroness Hilla von Rebay
New York City, N.Y.

Dear Hilla:

We are all attached to Roland [her nephew] and would receive him here with pleasure were it not for the fact that we are overloaded.

Even so, it might be better if he owed his presence here as much to you as to us. So send him on. The stipend for each member is $125.00 per month for the year and no part time participators. That however, will apply to him only part time and if you are hard up and feel you can't pay for him we will charge it to profit and loss.

We are all concerned about your strength--so needed at your best in the building of the *[Guggenheim]* Museum which really seems imminent at last after seven years waiting. The thing has about bankrupted us to date absorbing so much of our resources. But we are now hoping for an end to the financial burden as the actual building decreases it and increases in other ways our responsibilities. We will meet in New York for the Trustee meeting, February 4th--

May 31, 1952

Edmund Whiting joined the Frank Lloyd Wright Foundation in June of 1940. The following is a list of projects and commissions on which, with other members of the Foundation, he was engaged.

1. Work on masonry of the Hillside Drafting Room.
2. Built furniture in rooms of Hillside Apprentice Quarters.
3. Work with others on models for Museum of Modern Art Exhibition.
    a. Broadacre City Model
    b. Cantilever Bridge Model
    c. Model of group of Usonian houses, Okemos, Mich.
    d. Model Gregor Affleck House
    e. Model Ralph Jester House (Martin J. Pence)
    f. Village Service Station Model
    g. Model St. Mark's Tower
    h. Walter Davidson Sheet Metal Farm Units
4. Projects and commissions worked on:
    a. Leigh Stevens house and adjuncts
    b. Crystal Heights Hotel, Theater, shops
    c. John Nesbitt House
    d. Arch Oboler House
    e. Florida Southern College Library

He left the Foundation in March 1941 to join the Armed Forces.

August 15, 1952
Aaron Green
Los Angeles, California

Dear Aaron:

Had just talked with Eric Bass before your good letter came. I always intended to get you to help down there but wanted to wait until we had them settled down. Glad you happened in. The plans as now revised are nearing the hundred thousand mark but the price still seems high indeed, as expected.

I don't think John Lautner is needed. While Lloyd is available it seems to me some of his contractors would be more familiar with my kind of work.

My plan is to budget the work--send Joe *[Fabris]* to superintend under your jurisdiction by occasional visits. This would be the best plan to save the 20% Contractor's profit. What do you think?

We should, probably, do a cottage for the Bauers. Why not? We are to do one now in Phoenix for Mrs. Boomer.

Go and see Bass soon and help iron out his difficulties if you can. If not, call me.

[Joe Fabris, a member of the Fellowship since 1948, is one of our staff. He supervised several Frank Lloyd Wright buildings. The one above refers to the shops on Rodeo Drive in Beverly Hills.]

March 31, 1953
N.A. Rubin, M.D.
Canton, Ohio

Dear Dr. Rubin:

Sending an earnest young fellow, here four years, eager to help you and give a good account of himself.

Terms: $50.00 per week, his board and traveling expenses while he is necessary and on the job. Name, Allan Gelbin.

June 23, 1955

To whom it may concern:

Allan Gelbin has been associated with The Frank Lloyd Wright Foundation for six years, from July, 1949 to the present time. For four years he was an apprentice under my direction and for the two following years he was superintendent in charge of the construction of three of my houses.

He has given a very good account of himself and I am happy to recommend him.

March 27, 1953
Joe Fabris
Beverly Hills, Ca.

Dear Joe:

Unit lines should be V cut on all slabs. Put in color.

Until things get going there you would better come and put in a week here on the model [for H. C. Price Tower, Bartlesville, Okla.]. Kenn needs help.

We can then talk over what has come up there.

October 28, 1952
Local Board 115
Newtonville, Mass.

Gentlemen:

We respectfully ask that Grattan Gill be allowed to continue his training in Architecture in The Frank Lloyd Wright Foundation.

The Foundation since 1932 has been a cultural and educational organization under the laws of the State of Wisconsin. It is non profit and exempt from taxation by the United States Government. It is all accredited by the Veterans Administration and accordingly has trained some seventy five veterans.

Grattan Gill began his training on September 1st, 1952 and is doing very good work which should not be interrupted at this time.

A young Italian architect, Angelo Masieri, and his wife visited Taliesin in 1951. On their return to the East Coast, Mr. Masieri was killed in an automobile accident. As a memorial to her husband Mrs. Masieri commissioned Mr. Wright to design a student domicile and library on the Grand Canal.

April 9, 1953
Bruno Morassutti
Milan, Italy

Dear Bruno:

Glad you like the Venetian Opus. I do. Hope you can help us all see the building built. Lucky you are near.

In 1952 Edgar Kaufmann, Jr. and his father commissioned Mr. Wright to design an apartment building, called Point View Residences, for Pittsburgh, Pa. It was designed but never built.

December 26, 1952
Edgar Kaufmann, Jr.
New York City, N.Y.

Dear Edgar:

For some strange reason, now in the lap of the gods, I did not see your letter nor become aware that you had returned, in the plan case, the originals. I wondered why the delay. I asked a number of times if you had returned them and the tragedy of the mother's loss about that time allowed me to think you had no disposition to make of them just then.

But the changes you suggest are entirely reasonable except the single elevator. You see, Edgar, they are a combination self service and servant type, one allocated to each level. Not too much for such a building even were both at one level. When you make one of them you leave half the apartments to walk up a half flight or make steps between floors--12 stops. One half (or six families) (plus incidental service) require one such car as shown.

Think this over. It would be suicide to cramp convenient elevator lift in a building of this character.

We expect to see you and Senior here before long. All are hoping to welcome both of you here.

June 25, 1953

Dear Edgar *[Kaufmann, Jr.]*:

I am sorry to lose your cooperation on the magnum opus. Let's say it
is due to a misunderstanding--to wit: I thought you were to collate and
write the book with my assistance and it turned out that I was to write it
with your assistance. When the contract was signed this would not have
mattered so much.

But, choosing between writing about buildings already built and
building new ones--soon came along. Well, what would you say?

The second try at the apartment site is in acute final engineering
stage--improved. The area now, at $20.00 per foot, runs to $750,000.00.
The garage below should cost no more than $10.00 a square foot or
about $100,000.00. I've moved the garage off the rocks toward the mid-
dle of the lot where but little excavation is needed.

So there is no good reason why at last the Kaufmanns shouldn't be
able to build something well within the million you have to spend,
designed by myself. I've kept the important features of the design, being
myself unwilling to sacrifice the integrity of the thing as I see it--to further
reduce the costs by reducing the value of the enterprise as a whole. I
don't believe Senior wants that either.

Affection--give my love to Senior. We missed you both at the birthday
party.

N.B. The Price Tower (all face too) goes into contractual stage at 1½
million. Plus architect's 10% fee. 60,000 square feet more highly concen-
trated than your building.

July 15, 1953

Dear Edgar (Mr. Kaufmann):

I've notified father that the plans for Point View Residences are ready
to see, asking him to come. He asks me (calls me Mr. Wright) to send
them to him at Pittsburgh. But, Edgar, we never send out the originals until printed. Perhaps, if he is indisposed you can come see and if in general
o.k. we can then print them and let you take them on to him for discussion. I should think he would want to have my view of them. But, if not, I
can't insist.

If you are engrossed by your new project and you don't feel able to
come I will print them and send a copy to you. Or to him as you say. So
much better to discuss first impressions with clients, I find.

But what do you say--

December 30, 1953

Dear Edgars (father and son):

Herewith the fruit of much intelligent labor in behalf of your Pittsburgh residence project.

The first set (almost complete) may go on record for what it is worth. A pretty fine opus just the same, approved by Junior. I have included them as a reminder of our conversation concerning them at Taliesin West, in the draughting room. Wes present. Marked A.

The second, now completed, set--all engineering included. I felt the attempt to use steel was not only a failure but after careful study of the blueprints made by your Pittsburgh people concluded that not only did their steel proposition ruin the building but actually added about two feet to its height and considerably beside to the cost of the opus.

Therefore I went thoroughly into the reinforced concrete designing of the structure sure that results will be not only less expensive but permanent, requiring no upkeep during several centuries whereas the steel framing as designed by the Pittsburgh was not only wholly unsuitable but would have to be maintained continually after fifty years. Nothing Pittsburgh engineers did fitted the building and was more water over the dam for us. But, we are now ready for figures. You will note that I have reduced the depth of the foundation walls and garage area by pulling the building back toward the street. This loses us nothing, reduces the garage and bridge areas: cuts twenty six feet off the garage and bridge and sixteen feet off height of walls.

Square foot now of areas:

Garage area covered	5,500 sq. ft.
Garage area un-covered	6,300 sq. ft.
Total enclosed area in apartments	35,058 sq. ft.
Total enclosed area (cubic content)	322,877 cu. ft.

All engineering of Heating, Ventilating, Plumbing and lighting has been worked out as a basis on which estimates may be based and counter suggestions of various contractors considered.

Estimates may now be close and intelligently made; all uncertainties eliminated if contractors can see and read. Pittsburgh should have first go at the project but other cities should have a chance and no doubt many contractors in other cities would like to build so distinguished a building as this one will be. The plans will explain themselves and show you that nothing in your city nor any other can show anything so complete in eminence or elegant and luxurious to live in.

Your own quarters at the crown are superb and should be worth $1,000.00 per month at least. You know your other prospects. They are all on a high-par, quite out of the Pittsburgh world, maybe. But I think not. Luxury for the "ruling classes" climbs steadily. What was $100 worth ten years ago has to be $350 worth today, etc., etc.

Which brings us to the fact that our own Foundation enters the New Year considerably over $50,000.00 in the red. Creditors to the right of us and to the left of us.

The New York show was a triumph of hope over experience. We won but at an awful cost. Now the City of Los Angeles pays for the show--will build to house it and pay all expenses if the city can have five weeks off on the traveling of the show to the Orient.

The S.R.G. Museum has not yet settled with us but seems officially inclined to hold all gate receipts to pay expenses which all other museums have had facilities free to provide to the exhibitor. The S.R.G. Museum had less than nothing at all. All had to be made. We made it and now will see if we have stumbled over one corner of the Guggenheim fortune. Your relative, Arthur Kaufmann, came to the show with his Pittsburgh architect on some Philadelphia project--was very nice and congratulatory, of course.

Museum attendance astonished everyone except me. Daily attendance often over 3,200 from about thirty days. Total paid admissions at fifty cents each, 78,000. (Sundays over 4,000). Owing to newspaper strike lost about a week as show was scheduled to close November 20 and no means to inform them. Still many kept coming. Catalogues sold fourteen thousand.

This should not leave me holding the bag but I am holding it until the trustees meet next month. We can hardly expect such success in L.A.

There should now be no great difficulty, only some prospecting to find firm bids on your opus within the one million we were aiming at. Reductions in quality can be made. Oak wood floors are everywhere on apartments. The Price Tower, much more expensive due to larger more expensive perimeter space enclosed is under complete contract for $21.00 per sq. ft. Exclusive of Architect's fees. They are never included in costs as figured. If your minds have not changed again and you still wish to proceed with the project you are now in possession of complete plans and specifications to not only secure reliable comparative estimates but to build the building according to design as approved by you.

I made it clear to Junior (who may not have passed it to Senior) that we do not do speculative planning and our services are not conditional.

We do try our level damndest best however to meet the wishes, hopes and faith of our clients, both good and bad. There should be perfect understanding about this by this time.

I do not think it fair that gratitude for foundation aid to foundation exhibitions should be held either in feeling or in fact against our services to it as an architect.

Faithfully, gratefully and with affection as ever.

The bridge referred to in the next letter is a design Mr. Wright made in 1949 for a crossing of the southern bay, near San Francisco. If the bridge had been constructed, it would have been the largest single reinforced concrete span in the world.

July 27, 1954
Aaron Green
San Francisco, California

Aaron: can you place the Bridge model temporarily in San Francisco—must be moved within a week or so—

In 1951 Mr. Wright began work on a series of house designs he entitled "Usonian Automatic." It was a new concept in concrete block designed, refined and developed from the work done in California in the 1920's. This block system, described in The Natural House, *was intended to let the client, whenever possible, assist in the construction of the house and thereby keep the cost of skilled labor to a minimum. Charles Montooth and former apprentice, Arthur Pieper, went into partnership as contractors to launch this type of home. The first one was built in Scottsdale for Arthur's father.*

Walter Bimson, president of the Valley National Bank, commissioned a housing project for Phoenix in which Mr. Wright used the same block technique. The housing project was not built.

September 19, 1955

Dear Charles *[Montooth]*:

Arthur is on the way back and we will form a group to do many block houses, Usonia style. Arthur's father's house will be a good one. Then Bimson's group, etc., etc.

July 11, 1955
Mr. Bruno Morassutti
Milan, Italy

Dear Bruno:

The article looks excellent. Tell the Masieris that I will modify the facade to remove the neighbor's objections if they will write to me and tell me just what is needed. I think it can be managed with no loss to the opus.

[*The city fathers of Venice admired the scheme for the Masieri Memorial, said that nothing so appropriate to their city had been built in the last several hundred years. But objections to any "modern" building on the historic Grand Canal came from the Committee on Tourism, which brought pressure against the project and it was abandoned.*]

Of all the buildings Mr. Wright built during his long, creative life, the Solomon R. Guggenheim Museum was markedly the most difficult. The concept of a spiral building, growing larger as it rose, with gently sloping walls for exhibition surfaces, lighted by a continuous running band of skylights, and an open well bringing light from above down into the entire building, were ideas too advanced to be understood by most people, least of all by the 19th century building codes of New York itself. Artists doubted that the space provided for exhibition would be appropriate to their works. Many feared that the building would overpower their paintings.

"It is not to subjugate paintings to the building that I conceived this plan. On the contrary, it was to make the building and the painting an uninterrupted, beautiful symphony such as never existed in the World of Art before." he wrote.

Even during the years the building was in construction, the headaches continued. Mr. Wright was beset by continuing doubts, arguments, and ignorance on the part of artists, of some of the Museum's staff itself, and the director. The building, to this day, is still being victimized by lack of understanding. The shaded courtyard separating the main gallery from the office "monitor" has been ruthlessly blocked in to make a shop and restaurant. The charming little cafe he designed for the building on the main level has been conscripted for mere storage. Perhaps someday the building will be understood, stripped of its recent damaging changes, restored to its original concept, so that it may be used and enjoyed as it was intended.

MARCH 4, 1956
WILLIAM WESLEY PETERS
PLAZA HOTEL, NEW YORK CITY

CONVEY TO FRIEND HARRY GUGGENHEIM THIS THOUGHT FROM ME. SINCE THE CHANGES SUGGESTED BY SWEENEY INVOLVED NO SPECIFIC CHANGES IN THE STRUCTURE IN ANY CASE, WHY NOT DEFER THE CHANGES IN THE USE OF THE BUILDING, UNTIL IT IS CLEARLY AP-

PARENT WHAT TO CHANGE. I DO NOT THINK SWEENEY UNDERSTANDS THE BUILDING, AND UNTIL THEN HE IS NOT COMPETENT TO DECIDE AGAINST THE ARCHITECT. ALL THAT IS SUGGESTED IS POSSIBLE BUT NOT SEEN AS DESIRABLE. A NEW DIRECTOR MORE IN SYMPATHY WITH SOLOMON R. GUGGENHEIM BEQUEST MAY FEEL DIFFERENTLY. WHY, AFTER THE PRESENT ARRANGEMENT WAS MADE ESPECIALLY TO SUIT SWEENEY, DOES HE NOW WISH TO TURN THE AFFAIR UPSIDE DOWN AND DESTROY THE BUILDING. WE SEE NOW HE IS COMPLETELY INCOMPETENT TO READ A PLAN. BY WHOSE ADVICE IS HE NOW ACTING?

MARCH 13, 1956
WILLIAM WESLEY PETERS
PLAZA HOTEL, NEW YORK CITY

WES:

ALL RIGHT, IF SO, CHANGE ELEVATOR. TRY TO SEE AND EXPLAIN TO HARRY AS WELL AS YOU CAN THAT TO BLOCK OFF THE RAMPS WOULD UTTERLY SPOIL THE USE OF THE MUSEUM, WHICH IS ITS BEAUTY. EXPLAIN TO THEM THAT THERE IS A DEFINITE PATTERN OF EXHIBITION, AS THE IDEA OF THE MUSEUM, AND SWEENEY HASN'T GOT IT. I WOULD LIKE TO COMMISERATE IF I WERE ASKED, AND MIGHT DO WITH THE MODEL AT HAND. PERHAPS MODEL SHOULD NOW BE REVISED AND INSTALLED AT THE PLAZA. I ASSUMED ALL THIS VIRTUE WAS KNOWN TO THE TRUSTEES AND TO SWEENEY.

[Harry Guggenheim, nephew of Solomon R. Guggenheim, was president of the Board of Trustees of the Museum.]

MARCH 16, 1956
WILLIAM WESLEY PETERS
PLAZA HOTEL, NEW YORK CITY

THE MUSEUM IS ITSELF A LIGHTING PROJECT. IT EXISTS IN THE TOP LIGHTED END OF THE LITTLE KITCHEN, TALIESIN NORTH. MIRACULOUS OVER PERPENDICULAR WALL, SO EVEN BETTER ON WALL SLANTED. UNCLE SOL SAW THIS. WHY NOT GIVE US A CHANCE TO SHOW? MEANTIME A LINE OF OUTLETS CAN BE RUN FURTHER IN BUT FAR AWAY FROM THE SKYLIGHT FOR POSSIBLE USE BY SWEENEY. EXTRA EX-

PENSE OF COURSE. YOU SEE IN THIS A DUEL BETWEEN UNCLE SOL'S
MAN, MYSELF, AND HARRY'S MAN, SWEENEY. UNCLE SOL'S MAN HAS
NOT MUCH CHANCE BECAUSE UNCLE SOL IS DEAD. TRUE COM-
PARISON OF LIGHTING ONLY POSSIBLE WHEN BUILDING IS BUILT.
HAVE WIRED HARRY AN APOLOGY.

*The Lenkurt Electric is a large industrial building that was designed for
San Mateo, California. Aaron Green acted as Mr. Wright's West Coast
representative throughout the various stages of the design. The full set of
working drawings was completed in 1956, but the work was never built.*

March 3, 1956

Dear Aaron:

The complete Lenkurt is being sent to you to deliver to them. The first
half of commission is now rendered. A check for the first payment as
agreed now due. A letter from them accepting them will bring the
clerical plans within a reasonable time.

February 16, 1957

Dear Aaron:

For some reason the Pace people sent you a copy of the communica-
tion concerning a model of the main light fixture. Kindly take up the matter with Lenkurt and see if they will authorize the expense. All experts are
an ass.

February 12, 1958
Lenkurt Electric Company
San Carlos, California

Gentlemen:

I am willing to share the change in original conditions and we accept
your offer of settlement. But, my dear Lenkurt, the fault is not wholly

ours. Lenkurt shared in most of the delays. When the balance of the building is built--as I understand it--Lenkurt will pay the balance. I have no thought concerning my services to Lenkurt other than they have everything satisfactory to them. No easy proceeding as things go on or have gone.

So let's wipe the slate for the time being and agree that another check for $35,840.00 winds up the final payment up to supervision of construction. May this check reach us soon as a condition of this agreement? We are conscious of now having fulfilled our present plan obligation to "Lenkurt".

But should anything turn up which requires further attention, we will try to go along within reasonable limits of the scope of the original intention as recorded.

I have never wrangled with a client over fees. I know your integrity and that you believe your position just. The affair stands at that figure. The check you send is almost absorbed by our debts connected with services.

N.B. As for the use of the plans and supervision in case I pass out--the Foundation I leave behind me will be as able to perform to your satisfaction as any other service you could obtain. No legal complications can develop in the circumstances.

March 4, 1959

Aaron Green was in charge of supervising the Marin County Civic Center in San Rafael, California. The State Fair scheme was part of the overall Marin plan.

Dear Aaron:

I am absorbing the first payment on the State Fair scheme--but next payment will divide. I suppose the "third" should be taken out of the fee after reasonable deduction for cost of drawings? Or what have you? We are just between hay and grass all around.

Thanks aplenty for the beautiful blue rug which came a few days ago-- the color is a remarkable blue. The office gains a new dignity.

My best to you all--

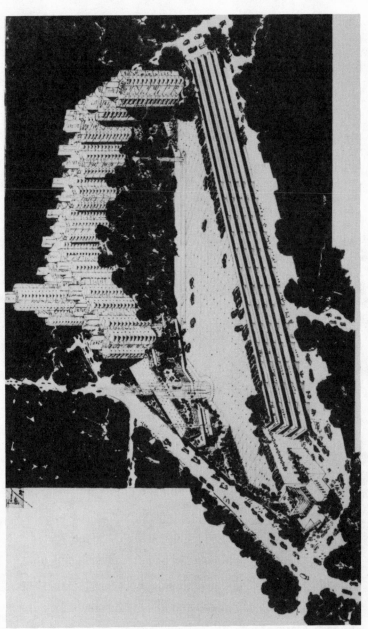

Project: "Crystal Heights"   hotel, apartments, shops and theatre   Washington, D.C.   1939

Project: Masieri Memorial   Grand Canal, Venice   1953

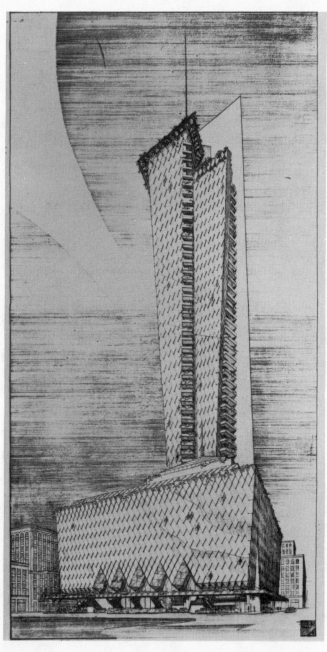

Project: Rogers Lacy Hotel   Dallas, Tex.   1946

Project: Community and Civic Center, Pittsburgh Point Triangle, scheme #1
Pittsburgh, Pa.   1947

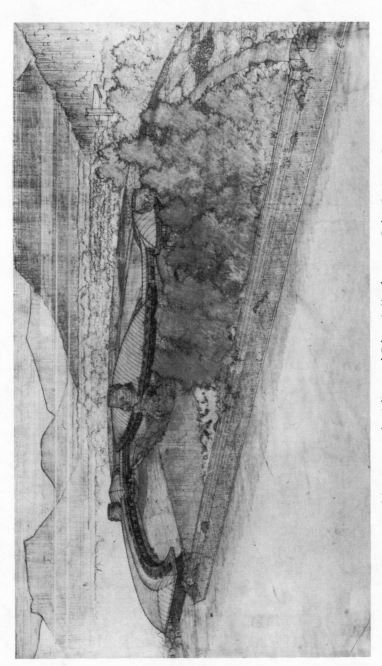

Project: "Boulder House" for Lilian and Edgar J. Kaufmann   Palm Springs, Ca.   1951

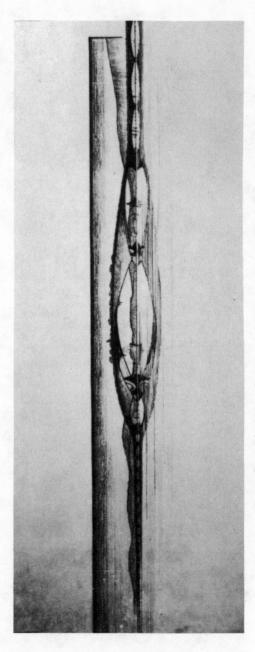

Project: "Butterfly Bridge" for the Second Bay Crossing   San Francisco, Ca.   1949

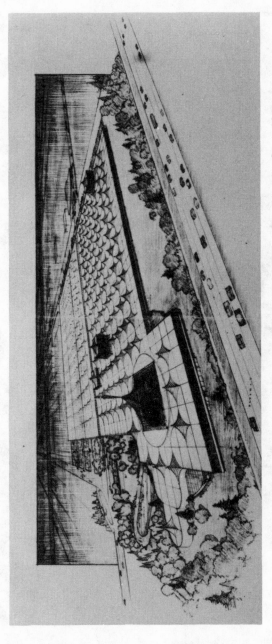

Project: Lenkurt Electric, office building and factory   San Mateo, Ca.   1955

Mr. and Mrs. Frank Lloyd Wright   Taliesin   1955

VI

LETTERS FROM APPRENTICES

In 1952, Mr. Wright sent a letter to many of his former apprentices asking them to a make a statement "about our work as a factor in your educational experience." Their replies explain the effect that the Taliesin Fellowship had upon them and show the harvest of their time spent at Taliesin.

July 29, 1952

Back in 1930-31 when I was an honor student at the University of Cincinnati, which is supposed to be one of the leading schools of Architecture in the U.S., I found the school far from satisfying my natural desire for real creative Architecture.

When my opportunity came to go to Taliesin, my great longing was satisfied.

Now I have gone out of Taliesin as a disciple and spread the "gospel" of an organic Architecture in Cincinnati and surrounding cities.

Everywhere I am recognized as one of the leading modern designers and always the Taliesin Fellowship is given credit for my early training, and I have been given credit for having understood the greatness of the message that Taliesin (deriving its spirit naturally from Frank Lloyd Wright) had, and has, to offer.

Sincerely,
ABROM DOMBAR
Cincinnati, Ohio

July 24, 1952

I was in the beginning of my work at Yale University in New Haven, Connecticut when first we learned through the press that the Taliesin Fellowship would open as a school for Architects, and it became my privilege to be one of the first of many students selected. It was my privilege to experience this architectural training, and, over the years, to watch many others come to Spring Green for similar work, (of a kind and quality, incidentally, that is available nowhere else in the world) and then go on to practice their profession in all parts of the country.

In my own case, the experience and training of the Taliesin Fellowship has been of inestimable value to me in securing my Architect's license, in my work during the war as special camouflage consultant to the War Department, as special lecturer on Interior Architecture at Northwestern University, and in developing and continuing an architectural office and practice here in Woodstock and in Chicago.

I might add that quite apart from the architectural training received at Taliesin, I owe a great personal debt to the Fellowship and to Mr. Wright for monetary scholarships accorded at a time when they were so needed for the completion of my training. And I know this same help was made available to other students who now are successfully practicing their profession throughout the country.

Sincerely,
WILLIAM B. FYFE
Woodstock, Illinois

June 18, 1952

I, Henry Klumb, at the age of 22, in the summer of 1927, finished my architectural studies at Cologne, Germany. It was the custom that after graduation young men would seek guidance by attaching themselves to architects of outstanding ability and achievement, to prove and test the knowledge gained in school.

The choice of Ateliers or place to continue study was great and varied in Germany, in Holland and in France, but most ardently desired was the chance to study at Taliesin, to work with Frank Lloyd Wright. In Europe, at that time already Frank Lloyd Wright's work was considered, by outstanding architects and critics, the new and basic philosophy of the most advanced architecture. In Germany his work was accepted as an American contribution to European culture. Thru good circumstances I was able to get to the United States and felt fortunate and privileged to be admitted to Taliesin, to continue and broaden my architectural education in a surrounding where work was devoted to the culture of architecture as part of life and man, to achieve the highest in human endeavor. Nearly five years, from January 1929 to September 1933, I studied and worked with Frank Lloyd Wright. During that time many young men of many lands and several continents shared with me the experience most valued by young architects. Most have returned to their native lands. Some have been lost during the recent world conflict. Those I know of are in high government positions, the others are producing work of merit.

I stayed in the United States and have worked in several states. I have been planning architect for the City of Los Angeles. The work I did in urban redevelopment was published in Henry Churchill's book, "The City is the People," and called, "The New Approach."

Today I am practicing architecture in Puerto Rico, a United States possession, and an island rapidly developing. I have done planning for Puerto Rico and Caracas, Venezuela, and have designed and built many buildings during the last eight years. Mr. Wright's influence, my association with the men he attracted, has given me the basis to develop a creative energy to meet the problems inherent in planning and architectural work of greatly varied scope.

That Frank Lloyd Wright's influence has and still is greatly affecting and guiding me with always renewed vigor, I admit proudly. To what extent this influence manifests itself in the work I have done is hard for me to tell. This judgment I will leave to others, and herewith attach an article written by the art critic of the New York Times who has recently visited Puerto Rico and seen my work.

HENRY KLUMB, Architect
Puerto Rico

June, 1952

I would like to state that the six year period spent as a student with Frank Lloyd Wright was the most important experience of my life.

In the principles of Organic Architecture I have found the basis of my life work. I believe, with others, that Mr. Wright's work in Architecture being given to students at his Foundation, is the greatest single contribution to American culture and Architecture today.

Now practicing successfully in Los Angeles, California, and having designed over 200 buildings, I know, and am grateful for, the value of the training we were given in the actual handling of materials, as well as the inestimable value of the principles we were taught, that was the reason for the founding of the School.

> Sincerely yours,
> JOHN LAUTNER
> Hollywood, California

June 16, 1952

This is my personal testimony of the immeasurable benefits I received from having been one of the apprentices at the Taliesin Fellowship.

The success I enjoyed in my architectural practice in China and the fact that I am at present among those participating in designing and building the world capital of the United Nations at its headquarters in New York, I unreservedly attribute to the sound outlook on life and architecture given me by Mr. Frank Lloyd Wright.

The inspiring contact with the great master was made available to me by the existence of the Taliesin Fellowship.

> YEN LIANG
> New York City

June, 1952

I was a member of the Taliesin Fellowship from 1935 to 1937. These were most difficult years for architects. When other architects were thinking mainly of how to survive themselves, Mr. Wright was planning for the future of American Architecture by educating the young men coming up.

While many of the members of the Fellowship contributed what they could, no one contributed as much as Frank Lloyd Wright himself. In my own case, it would have been completely impossible for me to attend this or any other school had it not been for Mr. Wright's generosity. In actual fact, far from realizing any profit from my presence at Taliesin, he was actually supporting me, giving me a home, and priceless education in addition.

As to the value of this education--again I speak from my own experience. I had a college degree in architecture and three years experience in building when I joined the Fellowship. I have been in the practice of architecture for fifteen years since leaving Taliesin. I feel, therefore, that my judgment is mature and objective. I can say unconditionally that all I know about architecture was learned from Mr. Wright.

Unquestionably my previous education and experience implemented this learning. But observation of students and young men in architecture shows me more clearly every day that the synthesis of facts and experience which can be obtained from study under Frank Lloyd Wright and contact with his underlying philosophy can not be obtained anywhere else in the world today. This is recognized by architects throughout the world, and I found in traveling all over Europe that Spring Green, Wisconsin, was known to architects everywhere because of the presence of the Taliesin Fellowship there.

A footnote on the value of this education to me: no other Columbus architect has been invited repeatedly to lecture on architecture for the School of Fine Arts at Ohio State University; no other Columbus architect has been invited repeatedly to lecture on architecture at the Columbus Gallery of Fine Arts; and no other Columbus architect has been invited to Stanford University to deliver a series of lectures on architecture.

I attribute all these circumstances to the illumination of my thinking brought about by being an apprentice to Frank Lloyd Wright. This recognition accorded me is not unique. I have found similar recognition being given to other former members of the Taliesin Fellowship throughout the Country.

In all my sincerity,
NOVERRE MUSSON
Columbus, Ohio

June 20, 1952

As one who received the best part of my training for the practice of Architecture at Taliesin I should like to evaluate for your consideration the importance of the work going on at Taliesin.

First let me say a word in qualification of myself. I am an Architect licensed by the State of California since 1941 practicing in San Francisco and have designed and built fifty or more projects of something over ten million dollars value. In six national competitions I have received honors-- three first awards including that of the American Institute of Architects for distinguished residential design. From this record you may judge the merit of the training work being carried on by the Taliesin Fellowship. As the form of apprentice training is all but lost to our time, Taliesin is unique in its direct experience "learning-by-doing" type of training. There is no other school in method of training like it in the world. But important as this method of training is, it is the content of the training rather than the method which makes Taliesin the most important place in architecture in the world today. This is because the training is based upon the most significant architectural work of our times. This work is the physical evidence of processes of thinking which have not existed for architecture for many centuries. Actually Architecture had become almost a lost art in the 19th century. Certainly it was a most confused art as any one can see from the gingerbread and wooden lace work on the imitation palaces that we have inherited from our grandfathers. The inventions of countless new materials and methods have further complicated the confusion. Never, at any time in history was there greater need for clear thinking and leadership in the field of architecture (as in all other aspects of life as well). All the great developments of our time come from the huge experimental laboratories of industry or government with sponsorship running into the billions of dollars.

Architecture which in effect is the environment in which we live, which, as I pointed out our grandfathers built for us and which we in turn are building for our children and our children's children, Architecture needs most urgently such developmental laboratories as may clarify for a confused world the possibilities of the future; certainly the Taliesin Fellowship is one of the most important Schools of Architecture anywhere today, as evidenced by the enrollment from Foreign Countries and the interested visits of distinguished people from all over the world.

Very truly yours,
F. L. LANGHORST
San Francisco, California

June, 1952

This letter comes to you from an Architect who had the rare fortune of being with green valleys, tall grass and wonderful people of your country for almost four best years of my life. You will be proud to hear that Spring Green and vicinity of your county is well known world over as a cultural pilgrimage to all whom Democracy and freedom is so dear and would give anything to preserve them. It is needless to point that all this honour and respect for such a recognition goes to one truly great man of our times, Frank Lloyd Wright.

Work of the Foundation Fellowship of Mr. Wright is an unique endeavour in Education of Master Builders and its roots and branches are spread all over the world. At one time or another seventeen different nations have sent their cultural missionaries to Taliesin. To us the Orient, Mr. Wright is a prophet with a great deal in common with Lord Buddha, Lao Tze, Tagore and Mahatma Gandhi. Young men in Architecture in India have long been carrying around Mr. Wright's books like sacred Hindu scripture. I have travelled extensively in Europe and in the East and believe me Sir, I have never experienced a single American and his works so much stimulatingly discussed as that of Mr. Wright's. It is so many times uncomfortable pointed out to Americans that everything America has in way of Art or other cultural value has a Continental flavour but here, right in your County is an Institution (for the lack of a better word) towards which not only Europe but the whole world has looked for guidance and leadership in Architecture for almost a generation. This truly American experiment in Education has set a pattern for many seats of learning in the world.

> Sincerely yours,
> MANSINHJI M. RANA, A.I.I.A.
> Delhi, India

In 1981, Mrs. Wright requested—as Mr. Wright had done in 1952—of many former apprentices statements of the value of their experience gained from the Taliesin Fellowship.

November 4, 1981

TO WHOM IT MAY CONCERN:

I owe almost everything in my architectural education and my career to Frank Lloyd Wright and to the Taliesin Fellowship.

> ANDREW DEVANE
> Dublin, Ireland

October 30, 1981

I can think of no life experience that has had a more profound effect on my architectural career than my time at Taliesin, and consequent exposure to the work of Frank Lloyd Wright, and to Mr. Wright himself.

Certainly, I would have found it extremely difficult, if not impossible, to acquire real insight into Mr. Wright's unique thought processes and approach to architectural design, without the Taliesin experience.

All my other educational experiences pale into insignificance in comparison, and I will always be grateful for the opportunity I enjoyed.

> Sincerely,
> FREDERICK LIEBHARDT, F.A.I.A.
> La Jolla, California

October, 1981

May I tell you briefly how much I cherish, after close to five decades, the privilege of being a charter member of the Taliesin Fellowship.

In 1932 I had just received a Bachelor of Science degree in Architecture from the University of Michigan. I knew that the academic training I had received hardly qualified me as an architect, as I knew little about how to design a building let alone build it.

However, my decade from 1932 until America's entry into the Second World War I had the great privilege of being an apprentice to my Master, Mr. Frank Lloyd Wright...

Now, after these decades, I look back as if it were yesterday when I would stand by in the delightful studio at Taliesin while Mr. Wright drew and designed without hesitation his famous structures at that time; Fallingwater, the Johnson buildings and others while I kept his colored pencils sharpened. And later I was sent off to supervise the construction of Fallingwater which exists today as the Twentieth Century most inspired example of American architecture...what better training could a young architect receive?

In brief, I must reiterate that the heritage of any student of architecture must be directed towards a creative achievement in architecture rather than that of an academic and technical education and that objective is achieved, as far as I am concerned, by the heritage of Taliesin...

Yours most respectfully,
ROBERT KEELER MOSHER
Marbella, Spain

November 10, 1981

As a Taliesin student of 1932-33 and 1948-49, I write in warm support of Taliesin's...architectural training program. Although I became a writer, not an architect, I was cited just a fortnight ago by the New Jersey Society of Architects for "outstanding contribution to the cause of architecture" through my many publications. Some of these were written under the name of Elizabeth B. Mock, and the publisher has most often been The Museum of Modern Art, New York.

Looking back over my work, I find that whatever it may have of lasting value must be ascribed to my Taliesin experience. Whether I was writing about buildings or bridges, towns or gardens, it was Frank Lloyd Wright's principles, as I gradually came to interpret them, that finally seemed to offer the survival-oriented approach.

Much more than Vassar College, from which I was graduated in 1932, and much more than the Museum of Modern Art, where I long ago served as Curator of Architecture, Taliesin has been my education and my nourishment.

Sincerely,
ELIZABETH B. KASSLER
Princeton, New Jersey

November 11, 1981

I joined the Fellowship in November 1950 and was immediately involved in a work and learning ethic for which I was not prepared. The ensuing years at Taliesin, however, have prepared me very well for my chosen profession, and they changed the entire focus of my life and the way I would live.

It is, I think, fair to say that just about everything at Taliesin is a "classroom." Most of one's time is used productively. I remember once overhearing an older apprentice saying to a younger one who was procrastinating over resolving some problem, "Just do it; you can always figure it out later." Taliesin clearly trained me to "do it."

As a young apprentice, it was difficult for me to understand why I had to work in the kitchen as a helper or on the farm or in the garden. What did these things have to do with being an architect? Why wasn't I in the drafting room working on the great buildings Frank Lloyd Wright was designing? When I finally was assigned to work on the drawings for a building, I brought with me not only the work experience of kitchen, farm, and garden but also that of having worked at Taliesin as a carpenter, mason, ditch digger, plumber, and roofer. I soon realized that the learning of drafting skills was not so difficult as I had thought, and the first-hand experience of having worked on the construction of buildings gave me a much clearer understanding of what I was putting down on paper.

What then of the non-construction assignments I performed? What purpose did they serve? As an architect I have designed in detail the kitchen of every residence I have ever built and have saved many owners the prospect of making major planning errors. My farming and gardening experiences have given me an understanding of the land. We had contour farmed and gardened. Those experiences have given me an understanding of nature, of how to use it and how it uses us, that I would perhaps never have understood otherwise. Most of all, they taught me how to work, how to be independent, and have given me a feeling of self-confidence based not on my ego but on the knowledge that I can achieve my goals through constructive thought and effort.

Very truly yours,
MORTON H. DELSON
New York, New York

November 5, 1981

It is difficult to express all my feelings about the great benefits and inspiration I have acquired, not only from you and Mr. Wright,--but from the entire program in your wonderful Taliesin.

Although I had completed my studies in Europe before coming to you,--it was the concept and the training of Taliesin, which prepared me superbly for all that I have been able to accomplish, when organizing a "Pioneer" Department of Interior Architecture at the School of the Art Institute of Chicago, where I taught for 26 years.

This program, based on the principles of Architecture subordinating itself to the forces of Nature, and thus utilizing its energy;--and the concept of planning: not for the outer appearance, but for the interior space; learning in turn to make this space utilitarian, but also exciting and beautiful,--these are some of the principles of Organic Architecture unique with the Taliesin School.

My gratitude is infinite. Through the spirit of Taliesin I acquired assurance of judgment of architecture, as no other institution could possibly give.

Very sincerely,
MARYA LILIEN
Chicago, Illinois

November 1, 1981

It is difficult, if not impossible, to adequately express in few words the great value of my years at Taliesin and beyond. Yet a few things come to mind.

For me, Taliesin was, and is, a great atmosphere in which to absorb all the elements I have ever needed to successfully and happily practice architecture and attempt to live a life along organic lines.

Aside from all the many architectural disciplines needed for successful practice, which Taliesin provided in more than full measure, I gained a love of the value of ideas, of youthful creativity, hard work, discipline, a greater understanding of myself and others, the world around.

After 4 years as a student I found myself at age 24, well prepared to go out and successfully build useful and creative buldings from scratch, as both builder and architect's representative. First, four beautiful buildings designed by Mr. Wright, and ever since, for 29 years, many buildings of my own design. A license came my way in Connecticut in those early days, as well as NCARB registration. I now have licenses to practice in 5 States.

Whatever I gained was far superior in all ways to other experiences I've had in architectural and other kinds of education through the years.

Taliesin was the beginning of a love affair with architecture which has never ended. I am most grateful to you and Mr. Wright and all of Taliesin for the many rich privileges afforded. All that you are out there gives much cause for hope for all mankind in a vastly troubled world. It is light and oxygen in what is often darkness, heaviness.

> Wishing you all well--
> ALLAN J. GELBIN
> Raleigh, North Carolina

October 27, 1981

Thank you for your letter of October 20, 1981. First may I say that the years I spent at Taliesin have been invaluable to me in my architectural practice in Iran, which as you know was registered and chartered to the Plan Organization to the Iranian Government. The study of Organic Architecture, the genius of Mr. Wright and the discipline and way of life which I became part of while at Taliesin enabled me to understand the relationship between culture and architecture and therefore endeavour to create designs which retained the essence of Persian culture and yet were totally modern and functional. I believe it was entirely Mr. Wright's teachings which made it possible for me to create such original designs which was the cause of my consulting office becoming one of the foremost in the country.

Our office was responsible for designing a number of hospitals including University of Isphahan; Teaching Training Hospital, 750 bed. Many teacher training colleges situated in different towns over the country. Office blocks including the central offices for the Iranian Oil and Gas Co. Also a few hotels and many private residences.

I cannot stress too strongly that the success my office enjoyed was totally due to the practice of the principles of Organic Architecture. I hope that the spirit and the way of life will continue and that students will always have the opportunity to come to the Frank Lloyd Wright Foundation and benefit from this unique experience as I did.

May I take this opportunity to congratulate you, Mrs. Wright on your continung efforts and wonderful leadership which is the inspiration to so many.

> With very Best wishes
> N. K. AMERY
> London, England

November 5, 1981

I have given much thought to defining to myself just what the Taliesin experience has meant to me and why it has been of such significance in both my professional and personal life.

I believe that for the young architectural student, Taliesin gives him the priceless gift of time..at perhaps the most critical stage in his life. It gives him an opportunity to look within himself and discover who he is, what he thinks, what his values are. It allows him to slowly absorb a myriad of experiences and to gradually determine what is, in essence, his personal philosophy--toward his work, toward society, and to recognize what his responsibilities are to both himself and to society.

During his time at Taliesin, he is exposed to many influences. To people from other backgrounds and other cultures, and to how they view life. He experiences the spiritual impact of living in the vast spaces of the desert, of living close to the earth, to the stars, to be surrounded by uncorrupted nature. He learns to live with a minimum of material necessities and he learns how to develop and use his own manual skills...to build, to plant, even to cook.

Above all, he is exposed to Mr. Wright's philosophy of the demands and responsibilities of the architectural profession. However conventional a student's training may have been before arriving at Taliesin, he learns to see and to think with a totally different vision.

At the present time, I am designing the smallest of contemporary houses, along with such other projects as city and concert halls, resort complexes, marinas, ski areas, large hotel complexes and such.

But, whatever the scale, from the largest to the smallest, whether contemporary western or traditional Japanese, always I am thinking "how to treat the space," of the quality of the space, of its relation to the people, the community, the environment.

This is my basic point of departure; it is fundamental to all of my designing. And for this I shall be ever grateful that I had the opportunity to live and to study at Taliesin.

Most sincerely,
KENJI ICHINOMIYA
Tokyo, Japan

October 27, 1981

My experience as an apprentice at Taliesin under Mr. and Mrs. Wright was the most important event in my life. It formed my understanding of human potentials as nothing else had done, and led to the best activities that involved me over the years, from the building of Fallingwater to work at the Museum of Modern Art in New York (1940-1954) and the eighteen years teaching at Columbia University. It also was the basis on which I could undertake the several publications on Mr. Wright's work with which I've been associated. Beyond all that, it has continued to mold my thought as a vital influence for almost half a century.

                                        With cordial greetings,
                                        EDGAR KAUFMANN, JR.
                                        New York, New York

December, 1933

   Taliesin is concerned with the impotence that is the consequence of the gamble in education, believing young America over-educated and under-cultured: sex over emphasized, present sex social differentiations absurd or obscene. Nor does Taliesin believe the "artist" has any special claim to divinity such as he arrogates to himself. As the usual "graduate" is educated far beyond his capacity, so the "artist" sacrifices manhood to a bag of tricks, a mere pose or seeming. Both are insignificant--there is no health nor any strength in them. Personality gets in the way of the quality of individuality genuinely divine in man and that relates him nobly to all men. The being that is unconcerned with seeming has found in our life little soil in which to grow. As the "American" people our ingenuity is unquestioned. Intellectually we function in the glittering generality pretty well and for certain specific purposes very well. But where the deeper needs of men are concerned (we speak of these needs as Art and Religion)--we beg or borrow or steal what we have and assume the virtue we have not. Nor do I doubt that, in the large, we have been cut off from the life-giving sources of inspiration by the very means we take to find and reach them. Take youth away from the ground, put growth on hard pavements and pigeon hole it in the city--and the first step has been taken toward future impotence. Herd youth in schools and colleges, textbook and classroom the growing period, and what have you but vicarious power in the hands and a cigarette in the mouth? Send the more self indulgent, egotistic youths to Art Institutes and again the vicarious life and the insignificant "me." Technique and nothing to do with it. Men of vision? Men of deep feeling? Men to create life anew and the strength to meet defeat in that cause? Not much of any of these qualities. Our youth runs more and more to journalese and the wisecrack. Stimulants an inevitable craving. And youth will have to function in fashion, the critical faculty stimulated with no valid basis for criticism; choice predetermined in various shallow or narrow grooves; personality more and more mistaken for individuality; mechanical horsepower or kilowatt mistaken for personal power. Noble selfhood run down into ignoble selfishness. The salt and savor of life that is joy in work soon runs stale in any academic formula whatsoever or in any attempt at "institution." A stale sap is the consequence. How can this knowledge-factory-education really culture any individual for the wrestle with machine-leverage owned by selfish interests, or encourage in man the interpretation of life in an era unprecedented in all the essential factors of the artifex? Education has gone on until, dropped from the present scheme of things, are these two great inner experiences, fructifying sources of good life--Art and Religion. Both, by way of education, have gone to seed. Seed on the barren soil capitalistic centralization has become where man-growth is concerned.

Architecture is the harmonious nature of all structure whatsoever, and a sense of valid structure in our culture is what we most lack. In steel, pulp, glass, and in the multiple powers of machinery and the basis for life they should bring with them, we have greater resources for new form than ever existed before and greater facility for failure. And it is a knowledge of Architecture in this broad, organic sense that is essentially not only the salvation of Twentieth Century life but it is the natural opportunity for a great culture. The very basis of our future as a civilization. An architect of an organic social order would then be our statesman. The poet and philosopher would be an architect of our spiritual life. The architecture of sound it was that intrigued Bach and Beethoven as music and this will inform our musicians. The architect himself on this natural or organic basis is necessarily the useful interpreter of the life of his era. Search for new forms is particularly his because we live in them and we live by them. If we had them we would be only too happy to live for them. Painting and Sculpture are features of such architecture. As for literature, the writer committed to the literal knows less of architecture in this sense--and unfortunately this writer is almost the only writer we have. By way of him the literal has invaded, confused, and corrupted the plastic arts. In all Artists must lie these deeper appreciations and realizations that, consciously or unconsciously, have always recreated, refreshed and lifted life above pleasure into joy. Our society knows pleasure but knows how little joy; knows excitement but knows no gayety; has lost innocence of heart in exchange for an arid sophistication that may debunk anything but can make nothing but machinery. Reverence is dead. Even reverence for money is dying. To machine-power we do reverence, still, but essentially human powers and human values are in the discard while we pretend to do them honor, expecting to get around to them again some day--somehow.

Well, Taliesin believes the day has come for Art in this more simple organic sense to take the lead in this thing we miscall "Education"; believes the time over-ripe for a rejection of the too many minor traditions in favor of great elemental Tradition that is decentralization; sees a going forward in new spirit to the ground as the basis for a good life that sets the human soul free above artificial anxieties and all vicarious powers, able and willing to work again as the first condition of true gen-

tility. Taliesin sees work itself where there is something growing and living in it as not only the salt and savor of existence but as the opportunity
for bringing "heaven" decently back to Earth where it really belongs.
Taliesin sees art as no less than ever the expression of a way of life in this
machine age if its civilization is to live. Yes we must go forward, feet on
the ground, with all our mechanical leverage made more simple and effective, to a new realization of human values in everything. By simple
measure of the man as a man and new standards of human values in
"success" it expects to measure the man for a nobler environment and
beget in him a better correlation of sense and factor. Taliesin is not a
back-to-the-land movement. No. Nor is Taliesin interested in art for art's
sake. Not at all. But means to go forward, feet on the ground, seeing art
as man's practical appreciation of the gift of life by putting his sense of it
into the things he makes to live with and in the way he lives with them.
When he makes them he must make them his own and make them worthy of his spirit. When he does that he will know well how to live with
them to greater purpose and with greater satisfaction of the demand real
men make upon themselves.

Taliesin

Frank Lloyd Wright